Sabres, Saddles, and Spurs

Also by the Editor

Old Abe's Jokes
Battle of Trevilian Station
Clash of Sabres—Blue and Gray
Civil War Stories
Ballads of the North and South in the Civil War
The War and Louisa County, 1861-1865
Train Running for the Confederacy, 1861-1865
Confederate War Stories, 1861-1865
Eyewitness to War, 1861-1865
Courier for Lee and Jackson
Raw Pork and Hardtack
My WWII Diary and the War Effort
Pacific Odyssey
and
The Award-Winning
Confederate Letters and Diaries, 1861-1865

About the Editor

After a distinguished career in the United States Air Force, which included a short tour in The White House, Colonel Walbrook D. Swank has devoted much time to writing about the Civil War. His grandfather, Thomas S. Davis, fought under General J.E.B. Stuart, Commander of the Cavalry Corps, Army of Northern Virginia, and was a relative of President Jefferson Davis. This is his fifteenth book. He is a member of Society of Civil War Historians and the Military Order of the Stars and Bars.

In recognition of his contributions to the preservation and promotion of our Southern heritage and history he has been awarded the coveted Jefferson Davis Medal by the United Daughters of the Confederacy.

The colonel holds a master's degree in American Military History and was awarded membership in the Bonnie Blue Society which is based on his scholarly research and published literature.

Sabres, Saddles, and Spurs

by
Lieutenant Colonel William R. Carter, CSA

Edited by
Walbrook D. Swank, Colonel, USAF (Ret.)

 Burd Street Press

This Burd Street Press publication
was printed by
Beidel Printing House, Inc.
63 West Burd Street
Shippensburg, PA 17257-0152 USA

In respect for the scholarship contained herein, the acid-free paper used in this book meets the guidelines for permanence and durability of the Committee on Production Guidelines for Book Longevity of the Council on Library Resources.

For a complete list of available publications
please write
Burd Street Press
Division of White Mane Publishing Company, Inc.
P.O. Box 152
Shippensburg, PA 17257-0152 USA

Library of Congress Cataloging-in-Publication Data

Carter, William R., 1833-1864.
    Sabres, saddles, and spurs / by William R. Carter : edited by
Walbrook D. Swank.
        p.   cm.
    Includes bibliographical references (p.   ) and index.
    ISBN 1-57249-144-2 (alk. paper)
    1. Carter, William R., 1833-1864--Diaries. 2. Confederate States
of America. Army. Virginia Cavalry Regiment, 3rd. 3. United
States--History--Civil War, 1861-1865--Cavalry operations.
4. United States--History--Civil War, 1861-1865--Personal
narratives, Confederate. 5. Trevilian Station, Battle of, Va.,
1864. 6. Virginia--History--Civil War, 1861-1865--Cavalry
operations. 7. Virginia--History--Civil War, 1861-1865--Personal
narratives. 8. Soldiers--Confederate States of America--Diaries.
I. Swank, Walbrook D. (Walbrook Davis) II. Title.
E581.6 3rd.C37   1998
973.7'455'092--dc21
    [b]   98-37686
                                                             CIP

To

Mary Sands Wingfield

Contents

Illustrations

ix

Maps

Acknowledgments

I am indebted, and express my sincere appreciation, to these contributors who helped make this work possible.

Mary Sands Wingfield of Ashland, Virginia for the war diary of Lieutenant Colonel William R. Carter, CSA.

Catherine Pollari, Eggleston Library, Hampden-Sydney College, Hampden-Sydney, Virginia and the Virginia State Library, Richmond, Virginia for making this war diary available.

Mrs. Frederick Brush of Gordonsville, Virginia for the picture of the "Gordonsville Receiving Hospital," now the Exchange Hotel and Civil War Museum.

The National Archives, Washington, D.C.

The Library of Congress, Washington, D.C.

The Archives Museum, The Citadel, Charleston, South Carolina.

The Museum of the Confederacy, Richmond, Virginia.

U.S. War Department, Official Records, Washington, D.C.

—Part I—

Introduction

This is the introduction to the exciting war diary of Lieutenant Colonel William R. Carter, CSA, of the 3rd Virginia Cavalry, Brigadier General Williams C. Wickham's Brigade, Major General Fitzhugh's Lee's Cavalry Division, Cavalry Corps, Army of Northern Virginia.

Colonel Carter was born April 22, 1833, in Nottoway County, Virginia, and graduated from Hampden-Sydney College with the highest honors. He later studied law, and at the beginning of the war he was a member of the law firm of Howard and Sands in Richmond, Virginia. He enlisted May 27, 1861 as a private in Company "E", Nottoway Troop, of the 3rd Virginia Cavalry and was later promoted to lieutenant colonel. He was frequently in command of his regiment and always fought it well. He fell, mortally wounded, at the Battle of Trevilian Station on June 11, 1864, the greatest and bloodiest all cavalry battle of the war. The colonel was found in an abandoned Union aid station and was taken to the Gordonsville Receiving Hospital a few miles away. He died July 8 at the age of thirty-one and is buried at his home, "Hickory Hill," in Nottoway County.

Colonel Carter, with his regiment and brigade, played a significant role in the Confederate victory in this battle in which he gave his life. Here, in his own words, he leaves us a very detailed, outstanding and action-packed legacy of his day-by-day experiences in the War Between the States. The diary begins with the first entry being made on July 27, 1862.

1862

1862

July 27th. Regiment still in camp.

July 28th. Everything quiet.

July 29th. The day very hot & everything quiet.

July 30th. It rained this forenoon. Regiment in camp.

July 31st. Rained this forenoon. The enemy ran in our pickets at St. Peter's Church to-night at 11 o'clock. The Regiment was mounted to give them a warm reception, but they did not advance.

Aug. 1st. Regiment in camp still.

Aug. 2nd. Moved to Hanover C.H. & encamped to report to Brigade all the stores & c. at "White House" having been removed.

Aug. 3rd. Regiment rested to-day, but ordered to prepare three days rations. Encamped at the same place.

Aug. 4th. Gen. Stuart, with one Brigade, consisting of 1st, 3rd, 4th, 5th, & 9th Regiments, and two pieces of artillery, marched towards Caroline C.H. and camped to-night on the road to Port Royal, four miles from the C.H.

Aug. 5th. Went in one mile of Port Royal and, learning that the enemy were moving from Fredericksburg towards Frederickshall, marched towards Fredericksburg and the 9th Regiment being in front caught eleven Yankees. Camped to-night near Dr. John Washington's. Private E.T. Riggins, Company A. Capt. White, was killed through mistake by a member of 9th Regiment to-night.

Aug. 6th. The 3rd Regiment was in front to-day. Starting early to-day, when we came near Massaponax Church, saw the enemy and the front squadron under Capt. P.R. Burkeley charged down the telegraph road towards Fredericksburg and his horse giving out, the command was turned over to Capt. G.D. White, Company A, who led the charge three or four miles, capturing upwards of forty prisoners and several wagons. The second squadron under Capt. Owen charged down the road towards Richmond and captured several wagons and some prisoners. The third squadron under Capt. G.B. Jones came up to their support an charged beyond, capturing prisoners and wagons. The enemy were advancing in line of battle and even bringing up their artillery, when Capt. T.H. Owen again came up and, charging them, enabled the wagons and prisoners to be gotten off. The enemy received them with a hot fire and then broke in confusion. In this affair private John Brewer, Townshend, and W.G. Wilkins, Company C, were wounded—Brewer through the thigh; Townshend through the leg very badly; and Wilkins slightly on the ankle. The Regiment captured to-day fourteen good wagons and eighty four prisoners. The 4th Regiment and the artillery then came up and shelled the enemy for some time, while our Regiment and all the prisoners and wagons, put in charge of Capt. F. Guy, Company D, were marched directly back. The Brigade camped four miles south of Bowling Green.

Aug. 7th. Reached the camp near Hanover C.H. this evening very much wearied and hungry.

Aug. 8th. Rested in camp to-day.

Aug. 9th. Received orders to move & camp out in the field.

Aug. 10th. Had preaching in camp by Rev. John McClelland private, Company D.

Aug. 11th. Quiet in camp.

Aug. 12th. Still in camp.

Aug. 13th. Everything quiet. Started from home in Nottoway to join the Regiment, though still unwell.

Aug. 14th. Nothing new. Spent the day in Richmond attending to some company business.

Aug. 15th. Lt. Col. Thornton and myself returned to the Regiment to-day from Richmond and, in a few hours after, we received orders to be ready to march. Moved in the afternoon and, crossing the Pamunky, camped late tonight in F. Scott's field in Caroline.

Aug. 16th. Marched this morning and camped tonight in Hanover just across the North Anna river.

Aug. 17th. Moved on and camped late tonight beyond Louisa C.H. Weather very pleasant and the country through which we passed was very poor and rocky, consequently our horses suffered a great deal for want of forage, water, and shoeing.

Aug. 18th. Left our sick men and unserviceable horses and went on and camped in Spottsylvania County.

Aug. 19th. Left camp before day and stopped, on the Fredericksburg & Orange Plank road for several hours and got breakfast. Then moved on and camped at Mining Creek, Orange County.

Aug. 20th. Left the camp early this morning and found the enemy near Kelly's Mill on the Rappahannock. The 4th Regiment being in front, caught several prisoners and killed one man. Tonight we camped very near Stone's Mill and were very hard up for something for man & horse to eat.

Aug. 21st. Gen. Longstreet's forces came up and shelled the enemy, who replied. Our Regiment came back to Maddens and remained dismounted in an orchard till evening, when we brought up the rear of Gen. Longstreet to Stephensburg. Reached Stephensburg very late at night and encamped in the town.

Aug. 22nd. Camped in Stephensburg, picketing towards Madden's and Raccoon ford.

Aug. 23rd. Moved into camp in woods near Stephensburg.

Aug. 24th. Col. Goode came up yesterday and assumed command. Hearing that a party of Yankees was in the neighborhood, he ordered me to take my company and scout in the direction they were reported and to make a dash at them, if prudent. Moved, as ordered, and found the report groundless. Returned to camp and Regiment moved to Brandy Station on Orange & Alexandria R.R. in Culpeper.

Aug. 25th. Still in camp at Brandy.

Aug. 26th. In camp still picketing.

Aug. 27th. Nothing new.

Aug. 28th. Everything quiet.

Aug. 29th. In camp at Brandy. Heard heavy firing towards Manassas and one deserter came in.

Aug. 30th. Had a heavy fight at Manassas to-day and yesterday. Enemy badly defeated, leaving their killed and wounded in our hands. The loss must have been 20,000 and themselves estimated at 17,000 killed, wounded and missing. Our Regiment still in camp at Brandy Station.

Aug. 31st. Rainy day and roads very bad—started for Manassas today and camped tonight near Warrenton with light feed for men & horses.

Sept. 1st. Clear and cool. Left the camp at 2 o'clock a.m. and marched through Warrenton taking turn-pike towards New Baltimore and fed at 10 or 11 a.m. near Gainsville. We then moved on and passed through the Battlefield, the enemy still lying unburied in large numbers. Saw large numbers of the 5th New York Zouaves lying dead and we had a large detail of the enemy's prisoners engaged under our supervision, in interring their dead. This was the most disgusting and sickening sight I ever witnessed—the puffed corpses of the Yankees & horses. Passed an immense line of ambulances, say 200 or 250 and 50 to 100 wagons of the enemy coming under flags of truce to carry off their wounded. Marched within five miles of Centreville and encamped tonight on the edge of Loudon County.

Sept. 2nd. Overtook Longstreet's and Hood's Divisions early to-day and passed them. Heard that Gen. Kearney had been killed the night before in a skirmish. Left the turnpike and moved to the left & fed our horses. After dark our Brigade made a dash on Fairfax C.H., capturing several prisoners. Passed a large house, on our right, in flames and late tonight encamped on the Alexandria and Middleburg turnpike, with nothing for man or horse to eat. Our Brigade put out pickets on all the roads to-night to pick up the enemy's stragglers, who were swarming from every direction.

Sept. 3rd. Moved nearly to Fairfax C.H. and fed our horses. Our men went to the Court House and remained all day, sending out

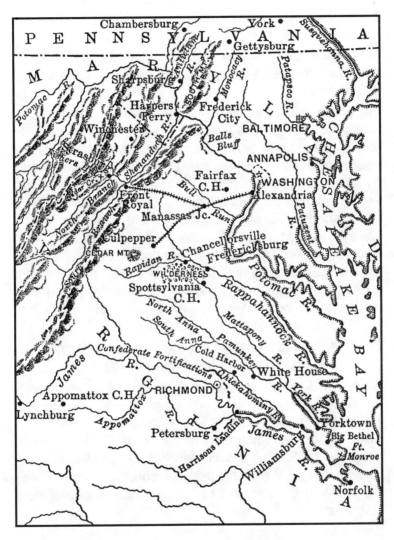

Field of operations in Virginia

scouts & pickets and sending to Fairfax Station for forage. Spent the day here catching and paroling prisoners and late this evening we moved towards Drainesville, encamping not far from the place tonight.

Sept. 4th. Moved this morning into field beyond Drainesville and spent the day resting & feeding our horses. Camped here to-night.

Sept. 5th. Mounted and marched before day towards Leesburg. A little after daybreak we fed our horses at Frankville on the pike to Leesburg. Remained dismounted in field near Leesburg several hours and then crossed the Potomac about 3 P.M., the boys gaily singing "My Maryland"-"My Maryland". We then marched towards Poolesville in Montgomery County and dashed on the place, capturing some thirty four prisoners and several horses & killed several. Part of the 3rd & 5th Regiments were engaged. The men supplied themselves here with boots, gloves, & hats at very low prices, the merchant taking confederate money without any hesitation. After dark we moved on the road up the river & camped near Missionary Chapel.

Sept. 6th. Moved by sunrise & fed this morning at Barnesville. Then moved on & camped to-night near Arbanna.

Sept. 7th. Moved this morning & crossed the Baltimore & Ohio R.R. at Monrovia. Passed through New Market & halted just beyond. Went on picket to-night on the road leading towards Hyattstown and the other portion of the Regiment on picket on the Baltimore & Fredericksburg turnpike. Spent a very good night, the people being reasonably kind & we having on hand a good deal of forage & stores captured at Monrovia.

Sept. 8th. Went into camp on the road from New Market to Liberty & had a very quiet time of it. The Marylanders dashed by on fine, fat horses and stopped to look at "Secesh". Here we had some recruits & heard pretty general expression of joy at our coming, as it suspended the operation of the Yankee Draft. I rather suppose their joy arises from the fact that they believe they will be left to do as they please & can stay at home unmolested by either party. Our boys bought some horses here.

Sept. 9th. Brigade moved early today & went in the direction of Hyattstown and arriving near Barnesville, found that several bodies of our Cavalry had had engagements with the enemy. Our Regiment went on picket to our left to prevent any flank movement from that direction. A small party of the enemy coming from towards Hyattstown & meeting our advance-guard under Lt. Hill Carter, exchanged several shots & retired. Late in the evening, all camped on Bennet river.

Sept. 10th. Moved through New Market & took the road towards Frederick and encamped near there, having crossed the <u>Monocacy</u>.

Sept. 11th. Remained here nearly all day & moved & encamped near a mill.

Sept. 12th. Left the camp early & camped near Catocton Mt.

Sept. 13th. Stopped at Highland this morning & drew rations for two days. Sent back sick horses and men to go on scout. Went back over the mountain by the same road we came & took nine prisoners, an ambulance, & several horses and returned across the mountain & camped near Myersville. The scenery in passing over this mountain was very beautiful; the country in the valleys, on either side, being in a high state of cultivation.

Sept. 14th. Gen. Hill's division had a severe battle with the enemy today on South Mountain and was overpowered by their heavy forces & suffered greatly. But Gen. Hood's division came up to his rescue & enabled him to withdraw. Our Regiment today moved through Smoketown & Myersville and spent the day resting & feeding our horses. Rev. M. McClelland commenced preaching to-day, but was interrupted by the sound of the Bugle to mount. The mounted marched to a position near Boonesboro & encamped for

SHARPSBURG
CAMPAIGN
Situation
Sept. 13, 1862

0   5   10
MILES

Lee's advance into Maryland

Clifford Dowdey

the night, being ordered to be ready to mount at 12 o'clock at night.

Sept. 15th. At 1 o'clock a.m. our Brigade was moved towards Boonesboro to cover the retreat of our army from South Mountain near that place. We passed up on the mountain beyond the town & remained until Hood's Division had passed back, when we fell back to the town of Boonesboro & put out a few pickets. The 9th Va. Regiment was in front and at 11 a.m. or 12 m. the enemy advanced infantry sharpshooters into the town under cover and also advanced artillery & cavalry along the turnpike. The 9th was ordered to receive the charge & the 3rd & 4th Regiments to wheel about and fall back out of the town. The enemy pressing, we charged him twice; but owing to the immense clouds of dust, the advantage the enemy had gained by our too long delay in the town, and their introduction of sharpshooters, we were repulsed & fell back with considerable loss to our Brigade. Lt. Jas. S. Christian, Company D., was killed; private Thos. B. Wainey, Company D, wounded & captured; privates John Boyd & R.H. Dabney, Company A., wounded; T.J. Cleaton, M.D. Richardson, R.L. Toone, & H.C. Omes, Company H., captured. Sergt. H.A. Meredith Company K. was thrown from his horse & captured. Lt. S.H. Ragland, Company C, was wounded in hand with a pistol. Sergt. E.H. Gordon, Company C, is missing & supposed to be killed. Lt. Hill Carter, Company D, was severely wounded & captured. Private C.W. Taylor, Company D, wounded in arm; privates Spencer Palmer & R.L. Banks, Company G. wounded and Lt. Col. Thornton, while gallantly leading the charge, had his horse shot under him. Total loss in this unfortunate affair were 1 killed, 8 wounded, 6 prisoners & 1 missing = 16. This same day a party of 6 men from Company B, who had been sent back from Highland with unserviceable horses, missing the Brigade wagons & falling in with Gen. Longstreet's wagons, were captured by a party of Yankee Cavalry escaping from Harper's Ferry, who cut off a portion of said train. They were captured near Williamsport & their names are as follows:

Sergt. Wm Lee, private A.G. Whiting, G.B. Herbert, Shields, L. Etheridge, & John Hall. This was an awful day for our Brigade, as the loss was heavy & the injury inflicted on the enemy must have been slight. Lt. A.E. Faulkes, a gallant member of the 9th Regiment, was killed to-day. To-day Gen. Jackson captured Harper's Ferry with upwards of 11000 men and large quantities of stores, the quartermaster commanding; medicine & ammunition. This was a great acquisition. We fell back from Boonesboro striking the Chesapeake & Ohio Canal at Dam no. 4. We then turned down the river towards Sharpsburg & encamped on our left wing next to Gen. Hood. Sent back pickets on the road we had come.

Sept. 16th. Our Brigade went out towards the enemy's lines & remained dismounted & in line all day. The enemy advanced & heavy skirmishing took place, which continued until after dark. We then marched to the canal & watered our horses & encamped, late at night, in an orchard near our camp of the previous night. Our camp was just behind Stuart's Battery, in range of the enemy's guns.

Sept. 17th. Left camp very early this morning. Heavy fighting all along our lines commenced this morning. Just as we were about leaving camp, a shell from the enemy's Battery struck the arm of Lt. Col. Thornton (just as he had mounted his horse), fracturing his arm in three places & necessitating amputation at the shoulder joint. From this he died at 1 o'clock on morning of 18th. Thus fell a gallant spirit—exemplary in all the relations of life! Brave, true, & faithful; eloquent & studious; a ripe lawyer, profound jurist, & estimable citizen. He was the pride of his county & the hope of his state. Corpl. T.J. Handy, Company H, was wounded in the leg by the same shell & his horse killed. The fight raged with fierceness during the day, and towards noon the enemy seemed to have the advantage, but, receiving reinforcements, we drove them back a quarter of a mile in the center and held the Battlefield. This was the severest battle of the war & the loss was terrific on both sides. The firing continued late to-night, but finally everything became silent save the groans of the wounded and the rumbling of ambulances & wagons bringing off the wounded & dead. There was no occasion for any Cavalry charge to-day & the fight was almost exclusively between Infantry & Artillery. Though our Brigade being moved from place to place & drawn up in rear of the Batteries to support them, we were very much exposed. Corpl. Hite, Company A, while we were in line to support a battery, had his horse killed and private C.W. Dunkly, Company A, was slightly wounded by a piece of shell. Encamped on our left again to-night, Capt. Thos. H. Owens, as senior Capt, being in command of the Regiment.

Sept. 18th. To-day was a day appointed for Thanksgiving by the President. There was a cessation of hostilities to-day & both parties were employed in burying their dead & bringing off the wounded. Our Brigade was employed all the early part of the day in collecting up the stragglers, (of whom there was an immense number), preparatory to our evacuation of Sharpsburg. Many of the enemy's wounded prisoners fell into our hands. To-night it was determined to evacuate the position, the enemy having employed the day in planting heavy cannon bearing on it. At 9 P.M. our Brigade was moved out to keep up appearances & cover the withdrawal of the Infantry & Artillery. Our Regiment took position on the suburbs of Sharpsburg and we remained awake with bridle in hand all night. At break of day, we fell in on the rear of the Brigade & marched rapidly to the Brick Mill ford below Shepherdstown in Jefferson County, Va. We halted one & a half miles from this ford & fed & rested. The enemy followed us up and cannonading commenced at 9 o'clock between the parties & continued during the day.

Sept. 19th. Early this morning the whole army finished crossing with the immense train of wagons and artillery, the only loss being one piece of artillery, which was disabled. Thanks to our Maker that this perilous & critical movement was performed with so little loss. No pen could describe the feeling of relief that every patriotic heart felt when our army arrived safely on the hospitable soil of Virginia! To-night we encamped on the farm of Mr. Marshall near Walpins X Roads. The enemy attempted to cross their infantry, but were driven back with heavy loss.

Sept. 20th. Went on scout towards Harper's Ferry and found that no effort had been made to cross at the lower ford. To-day the enemy again made the effort to cross at the Brick Mill ford, but were repulsed with tremendous loss—nearly a whole Brigade being captured, killed, & drowned in the river. About dusk the firing ceased & we encamped in a few miles of Shepherdstown.

Sept. 21st. Brigade moved towards Martinsburg collecting muskets that had been thrown away, and hurrying on the stragglers. This place is distant from Shepherdstown 10 miles. We encamped six miles from Shepherdstown.

Sept. 22nd. Moved the camp, picketing towards Shepherdstown & encamped in two miles of Martinsburg.

Sept. 23rd. In command of Regiment & sent 2nd squadron to report to Col. White. They returned at dusk having been engaged in provost duty. Capt. L.H. Owen got four days leave of absence to go to Winchester.

Sept. 24th. Still in command of Regiment and remained in the same camp shoeing & resting the horses.

Sept. 25th. Gen. Fitzhugh Lee was kicked by a mule & rendered unfit for duty. Enemy reported advancing by way of Shepherdstown and by order of Col. W.H.F. Lee of the 9th Regiment, acting Brigade commander. I moved the Regiment down to within one & a half miles from Shepherdstown. The enemy advanced to the opposite hill, skirmishing with our sharpshooters. After awhile they gave back & we followed them through Shepherdstown. Then encamped for the night & remained with the 4th Regiment on picket.

Sept. 26th. Returned to the same camp.

Sept. 27th. Moved our camp to Newcome's Mill on the Opequan Creek. On this day an order was issued by Gen. Stuart announcing Thos. H. Owen as Lt. Col. & W.R. Carter as major of the 3rd Va. Cavalry to take effect from the 18th Sept. 1862.

Sept. 28th. Regiment was ordered to Charlestown to support the force there under command of Major Massie of the 12th Va. Regiment. We bivouacked near the town on the turnpike leading to Harpers Ferry.

Sept. 29th. Early this morning we were called to have to meet an advance of the enemy from Harpers Ferry. They came dashing up, but being promptly met, they retired after exchanging several shots of artillery and a number of Carbine shots. They ran in all our pickets today at the Warm Springs X roads & towards Duffields. Lt. John Lamb, Company D, was surprised & captured this morning, on picket towards Harpers Ferry. This evening Maj. Massie relieved our pickets & Capt. Knott's company charged a party of the 1st Mass. Cavalry who came from Sharpsburg by way of Shepherdstown and were scouting about Duffield's Station on the Baltimore & Ohio R.R. Four of these were captured.

Sept. 30th. Still encamped near Charlestown to-day & part of the Regiment on picket. The enemy quiet.

Oct. 1st. The enemy made an advance to-day. To-night four pieces of artillery of the Richmond Howitzers came down.

Oct. 2nd. Still in camp in Charlestown.

Oct. 3rd. Moved to Leetown, Jefferson Co., Va., picketing from Duffield's Depot to Shepherdstown.

Oct. 4th. Still at Leetown & our pickets relieved by the 1st. Brigade.

Oct. 5th. Ordered to report to Brigade Commander & meet the Brigade coming to Stryder's Mill. Having asked permission to do so, we returned to our old camp at Leetown.

Oct. 6th. Went on picket towards Shepherdstown to relieve the 1st Regiment. Adjt. McClellan & myself dined with Ms. A.R. Botelair & had a pleasant time. Ms. B. loaned me Howe's History of Va.

Oct. 7th. Relieved by the 5th Regiment & returned to camp.

Oct. 8th. Remained still in camp & drew pay for my company—Co. "E"—for March & April.

Oct. 9th. One hundred & thirteen privates & eight officers were detailed from the Regiment to report to Gen. Stuart to go on raid into Maryland & Pennsylvania.

Oct. 10th. Col. Owen being absent, the command of the Regiment devolved on me. Remained quiet in camp today.

Oct. 11th. Still in command of Regiment & went on picket towards Shepherdstown to relieve 1st Regiment.

Oct. 12th. Being relieved by the 5th Regiment, we returned to camp & attended church at Leetown.

Oct. 13th. Still in command of Regiment & quiet in camp at Leetown.

Oct. 14th. The portion of the Regiment detailed to go with Gen. Stuart into Md. & Penn. returned this morning with horses very much jaded & broken down from hard service. This expedition taken from the different Brigades was composed of 1800 cavalry & two guns. They rendezvoused at Darksville, Berkeley Co., on the 4th Oct. & marched one mile beyond Hedgesville, where they encamped for the night. Early next morning they took up their line of march & about sunrise crossed the Potomac at a very rocky ford, capturing some ten or fifteen prisoners on the other side of the river, which prisoners were sent back under guard. Here they learned that a Division of the enemy, 10,000 strong, had just marched along the same road. But Gen. Stuart proceeded towards Chambersburg, Penn., giving orders to have details sent out, as soon as they passed the line, to capture all horses that were serviceable for artillery or cavalry. He reached Chambersburg & found the Home guards prepared to make resistance but sending them word that if they did not submit unconditionally & at once, he would shell the town, the commanding officer in the place very soon surrendered & the Gen. spent the night in the town with most of the command outside. This was a very rainy & disagreeable night, but such was the fear of the inhabitants that they readily

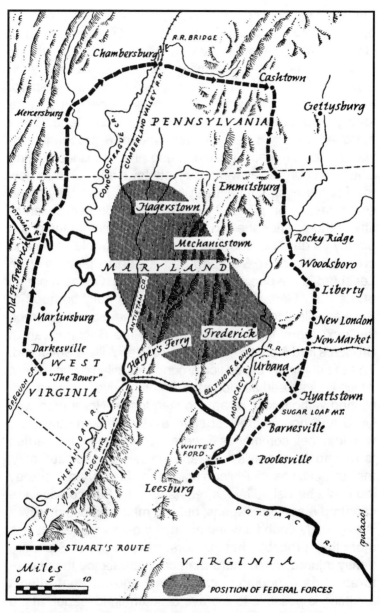

Stuart's 1800 Raid Chambersburg. October 10-12, 1862

Clifford Dowdey

furnished the soldiers, or "<u>rebels</u>", as they called them, everything they needed or wished to eat. On the morning of Oct. 11th. they set out early with the horses & other things they had taken—after destroying a large lot of sabres & such pistols as they could not bring away—towards Emmettsburg. Here our men met with a very cordial reception & were loudly applauded by the citizens of that place. They marched through Liberty & New Market & proceeded towards the Potomac without making any halt since leaving Chambersburg. They went by Hyattstown and cutting a new road to the river, struck it at White's ford. Here they found some cavalry on picket & charged, capturing some ten or fifty of them. After shelling the woods & such parties of the enemy as dared to show themselves, the whole command crossed the river & encamped a short distance from Leesburg in the direction of Snicker's Gap. On the morning of the 13th Gen. Stuart marched to the neighborhood of Snickersville. He there encamped for the night & returned the next morning to camp, crossing the Shenandoah at Snicker's ford & proceeding by way of Berryville & Smithfield. This extraordinary expedition around McClellan's whole army, which was spread all along the Potomac river, was accomplished without loss of any consequence. Not a man was killed and none were lost save a few drunken stragglers who lost their commands & were then left behind. It carried terror into the enemy's lines, and it is said on good authority, that the citizens of Philadelphia were frightened lest they too might be visited by the rebels. Some 1200 horses were captured & several wagons; but in a material point of view it is extremely doubtful whether anything was gained, as it is more than probable that the horses broken down & permanently injured would more than counterbalance those captured. This expedition conclusively showed that almost anything is possible to a brave & determined leader, at the head of good troops. It may not be improper to mention the high compliments, paid by our enemies, to the orderly & gentlemanly conduct of our troops, who respected private property under the extraordinary provocations of having their own homes devastated and female relations insulted by these same enemies.

Oct. 15th. Through mistake of Col. F.L. Roper commanding Brigade, was ordered on picket towards Shepherdstown & started with that portion of the Regiment that did not go to Pennsylvania, but we returned, the first Regiment having gone on duty.

Oct. 16th. Started on picket & heard that the enemy were advancing in considerable force under Fitz John Porter. After manoeuvering about for several hours, the Regiment was ordered to report to Gen. Stuart, who ordered us to go towards Charlestown to reconnoitre & ascertain the force of the enemy. On arriving near the Warm Springs cross roads & learning that the enemy had a picket at that place Capt. G.D. White, company A, was directed to make a dash at the picket with 40 men, while the Regiment was moved near to support him. Finding no picket, the party was divided into three parts & dashed down three forks of the road; one leading towards Shepherdstown, another towards Harpers Ferry, & the third towards Charlestown. Capt. White led the party towards Harpers Ferry & captured a Yankee provost captain. Private Jordan Christian, Company D, went within the enemy's lines after dark & ascertained that 5000 troops under McClellan had gone up to Charlestown during the day. He returned safely next morning & reported facts to Gen. Stuart who was much pleased with the whole affair. Returned at 11 o'clock P.M. to old camp at Leetown & sent out pickets. The night was rainy & disagreeable.

Oct. 17th. News this morning of an advance of the enemy this side of Kerneysville Depot, on the Baltimore & Ohio R.R., where they had a sharp skirmish with a small body of our infantry on yesterday. They advanced with infantry, artillery, & cavalry as far as Leetown, our Brigade gradually falling back before them. They remained here the greater portion of the day and then fell back towards Shepherdstown.

We pursued them with artillery & cavalry as far as Shepherdstown, capturing several prisoners. Having re-established our pickets at the same posts, we returned to camp at Leetown.

Oct. 18th. Remained in camp quietly, the enemy having all retired to the north of the Potomac.

Oct. 19th. Remained still in camp & attended church at Leetown.

Oct. 20th. Quiet in camp & went to Brigade headquarters to get a Bugler. Ordered to have roll calls three times a day & place out camp guard to keep the men from going out without leave.

Oct. 21st. Carried the Regiment on picket, Col. Owen remaining in camp.

Oct. 22. Returned to camp, being relieved by 5th Regiment. Nothing new today.

Oct. 23. In camp quiet. Today the 5th Regiment came from Stryder's Mill & encamped near us. Infantry moved back towards Winchester, having destroyed the Baltimore & Ohio R.R. by burning the sills & springing the rails

Oct. 24. Still in camp & commenced drilling in Sabre exercises on foot & in the squadron drill.

Oct. 25. Still quiet in camp.

Oct. 26. Col. Owen being sick, I carried the Regiment on picket. Weather rainy, cold, & disagreeable. Tonight a citizen of Shepherdstown, arrested by order of Gen. Stuart, was brought to me & sent under guard to Gen. Stuart at the "Bower".

Oct. 27. Returned to camp, having been relieved by 5th Regiment.

Oct. 28. Still in camp & drilled today. Were informed that there will be a review of the Brigade tomorrow by Gen. Stuart. Adjt McClellan went on detail to Richmond to get Bugles & Buglers. Another order late to-night to be ready to move tomorrow, with three days' rations, immediately after review.

Oct. 29. Review at 10 a.m., in field near Leetown of 1st, 3rd, 5th, & 9th Regiments (the 4th being absent on picket)—fine affair! Moved immediately afterwards through Smithfield, thence through Berryville, going down Berryville & Winchester, and Berryville & Charlestown turnpikes. Encamped near Snicker's ford on Shenandoah in Clarke Co.

Oct. 30. Crossed the Shenandoah at Snicker's ford & passed through Snickersville towards Aldie, thence taking the road towards Upperville passing through Bloomfield, Loudon Co., Va. Here we learned that a squadron of 150 Yankees had passed through the place a short time before our arrival. Brigade encamped near this place, our wagons having been ordered back from Snickersville to cross at some gap lower down.

Oct. 31. Went back through Bloomfield on scout towards Aldie. Marched through Union and Pathouse, the 9th Regiment being in front & the 3rd being next. Came upon a Yankee picket at Montville & charged it, killing & capturing nearly the whole. The 3rd Regiment getting in front, we pursued the enemy nearly through the town of Aldie, capturing a number of prisoners, saddles, & horses. The 3rd & 9th captured 67 prisoners & 2 negroes. Capt R.H. Walkins, Company K, was wounded on the head by a sabre, and Corp'l Hinton, company A, was wounded by fragments of a shell. Returned to camp near Union & found our wagons. Got Yankee sabre & saddle for myself. Many members of this Regiment displayed gallantry & courage in this affair.

Nov. 1st. Moved out at 11 o'clock to support our Battery beyond Union & check the advance of the enemy. The Regiment remained in reserve at this place. In shelling the enemy near Philmont, our Battery lost one man killed & 15 wounded. A caisson was exploded by a shell from the enemy. Killed & wounded a good number of the enemy. Capt. Walkins & Corp'l Hinton got furloughs to leave on account of their wounds. Returned to camp & ordered to be ready to move at day-break.

Nov. 2. Marched to Union to meet our advance of the enemy & sent on road to the right of Union towards Pathouse to check the enemy's advance that way. They advanced rapidly & in heavy force, so that our sharpshooters having been detailed by order of Col. Wickham, Commanding Brigade, we fell back toward our old camp at Newlon's Mill. The enemy continuing to press, we fell back gradually skirmishing & firing artillery at their column. Many shells burst over & around us, but fortunately our loss was small, J.B. Banon, Company A, was severely wounded in the thigh & G.C. Bacon, Company A, slightly in the hand, one finger being shot off. John T. Wilkins, Company C, was taken prisoner while carrying a dispatch. Encamped without fires near Upperville & sent 2nd squadron on picket. We supposed the enemy suffered considerably from our artillery and sharpshooters.

Nov. 3. Our pickets reported an advance early to-day. The enemy found carbines & artillery & advanced with a heavy force. We fell back gradually & in fine order, the foe pressing rapidly. Returned through Upperville and the 1st, 4th, & 5th Regiments took the road towards Piedmont; the 3rd & 9th took the one towards Basis & thence to Piedmont after dark, but finding the enemy had occupied the town, we turned to-night towards Markham Station on Manassas Gap R.R. Here we found the 1st, 4th & 5th Regiments, which had retired before the enemy. Private J.F. Parkinson, Company F, & W. Powell were wounded today. Col. Wickham acting Brigadier Gen., was wounded in the neck by a shell. Encamped near Markham to-night towards Manassas Gap.

Nov. 4. Moved out to Markham at 10 o'clock a.m. to meet an advance of the enemy. Ordered to go on to Barbee Cross roads to support 9th Regiment. We were overtaken by a courier reporting that one gun had been taken by the enemy, whereupon we whirled about to go back to meet them. Met by Col. Roper, Commanding Brigade, who told us the gun was not taken & to wheel about & to form in a field to our rear to support a gun. The enemy ceased to press & we came on to Orleans, Fauquier Co. & encamped 1½ miles from that place on road to Waterloo Bridge.

Nov. 5. Moved back to Barbee's X roads to meet the advance of the enemy; they advanced with sharpshooters, but would not charge. The 9th made a charge on them & so did Hampton's Brigade. Killed a considerable number of the enemy in this affair. After skirmishing some time, the Regiment was ordered back to Orleans with a piece of artillery to hold the road leading to Salem. At dark we retired to Waterloo Bridge and crossing, encamped in Culpepper Co.

Nov. 6. Ordered to mount and accompany a piece of artillery to Warrenton. Arriving there, we sent out pickets towards Salem & ourselves took position on the road to New Baltimore. Being soon informed that the enemy were advancing from Salem, sent out sharpshooters & draw them back. Then we commenced retiring on the road towards Waterloo Bridge & came upon a large force of the enemy coming to meet us, at Scott's Mill. Wheeled into field south of the road & the sharpshooters charged their sharpshooters & drove them from position behind a stone fence. We passed a raking fire from a battery of 3 or 4 pieces, but fortunately none were killed by the shells. Jos. B. Young, Company G, was killed by carbine while the Regiment was standing in the road waiting the movements. Of the artillery, W.E. Robertson, R.A. Gregory, Company A; G.H. Cole, L.S. Tucker & H. Ellington, Company C, were captured. This was an ugly scrape—force of enemy being 8 or 10 Regiments of cavalry, & with generalship & courage they ought to have taken or killed us all. Our Regiment acted with great coolness to-day & brought off their gun through fields & farm roads. We crossed the Rappahannock at Warrenton Springs & encamped near Jeffersonton, sending Capt. Field's squadron on picket. Several members of Company E. who had been cut off near Warrenton, while on picket, came up after running from the enemy through the woods.

Nov. 7. Last night was very cold—commenced snowing this morning & continued nearly all day. Pickets reported an advance of the enemy & we moved out to meet them on the road to Waterloo Bridge. Retired slowly before them and encamped on road to Culpeper C.H. near Rixeyville.

Nov. 8. Still in camp, enemy being quiet. Col. T.F. Goode's resignation was accepted to-day—T.H. Owen promoted to Colonelcy. W.R. Carter to Lt Colonelcy, & H. Carrington to major. A large number of our horses afflicted with <u>mountain</u> itch, or scratches, of very severe type.

Nov. 9. Still in camp, but moved back towards Culpeper C.H. for convenience of forage & fuel.

Nov. 10. Ordered to report at Rixeyville with several pieces of artillery. Brigade of Cavalry with 10th Ala. & 16th Miss. Infantry Regiments crossed the Hazel river at Rixey's Ford, driving the enemy back rapidly towards Amisville, Culpeper Co. Here we came upon a heavy force of the enemy's Infantry & in turn had to fall back. Our Regiment moved on the left of the road. We supposed that a number of the enemy were killed by our artillery, as several were found dead on the field. Regiment crossed the Hazel at Hill's Mill & picketed along this river—encamped on Rixey's farm near this mill. Private John Allen, Company G, fell in with the enemy while looking for our Regiment and was captured to-day.

Nov. 11. Quiet in camp & relieved our pickets to-day.

Nov. 12. Regiment still in the same place. I went to Culpeper C.H. to see Col. Roper, Commanding Brigade, and Gen. Stuart, relative to the large number of men at the wagons with horses unfit for service from the <u>mountain itch</u>. Gen. Stuart stated that he had determined to establish a sick horses camp forty miles in our rear & drill the dismounted men in the Infantry skirmish drill. Returned to camp late to-night.

Nov. 13. This morning ordered to scout in the direction of Amisville. By request of Col. Owen, I remained in camp with twelve sharpshooters to support, if necessary, the piece of artillery at the ford. He with balance of Regiment not on picket, went on a scout. Cap't, White, commanding advanced guard, charged through Amisville, capturing five Yankees, four horses & 23 saddles. Returned without any loss, having ascertained that a heavy force of the enemy was at Waterloo bridge. Picket not relieved to-day.

Nov. 14th. Regiment in camp today. Some large horses & dismounted men went to the camp to be established in Albemarle Co. under strict orders—men to drill there, on foot, as skirmishers. At midnight we received orders to be ready at day break to report to Col. Roper, Commanding Brigade at Jeffersontown.

Nov. 15. At day light moved towards Jeffersontown & found our artillery firing on the enemy from the hill south of Warrenton Springs. They had crossed & returned the fire heavily. Several of the enemy's wagons were burnt by our artillery & 4 or 5 of the enemy were killed. Returned to camp & ordered to keep Hill's Mill in operation, grinding flour for use of Brigade.

Nov. 16. Col. Owen being sick, I took Regiment on picket to relieve the 4th Regiment. Reserve encamped for night at Oak Shade church with everything quiet.

Nov. 17. Ordered to scout this morning towards Waterloo Bridge & Warrenton Springs. Moved the Regiment towards Warrenton Springs & sent a party under Jones, Company "B." towards Waterloo Bridge. Went within a few hundred yards of both places & found large force of Yankee Cavalry at Waterloo Bridge, with a picket this side river. At Warrenton Springs were pickets of the enemy every few hundred yards up & down the river. Returned to Oak Shade & reported to Col. Roper—was relieved by 5th Regiment & returned to camp at Hill's Mill.

Nov. 18. Moved to Jeffersontown to scout the enemy. Found them with two pieces of artillery at Warrenton Springs & after some exchange of shots, they fell back & we crossed, marched to Warrenton & encamped south of the town, without anything for man or horse to eat. Day very rainy & cold. At this place we captured a considerable quantity of sutler's goods & some prisoners. Soldiers generally supplied themselves with boots, overshirts & c. Found that the whole force of the enemy was moving towards Fredericksburg. McClellan reviewed & took leave of his army but a few days ago & Burnside assumed command. Army of the enemy is represented as being in a state of great disorganization in consequence of McClellan's removal. Enemy are laying waste the country as they go.

Nov. 19: At 11 a.m. moved from camp near town to Road leading to Fredericksburg. After remaining here two hours, fed our horses on fodder left by the enemy on road to Warrenton Junction. We then took the road to that place, capturing prisoners at all the houses along the road. Paroled 50 of such stragglers today, who doubtless put themselves in the way to be taken. From Warrenton Junction, 9 miles from the town, we marched at dark to Germantown, Fauquier Co. & camped without anything for man or horse to eat—men without rations now two days. Drizzly day & night. Found that Hooker's, Burnside's, & Sumner's corps have passed down towards Fredericksburg, taking all forage, cattle & c. as they went.

Nov. 20: Moved early this morning, our Regiment being in front & marched to Bealeton Depot on the O. & A. R.R. Sent 2nd squadron, Capt. Mathews Company "G," to charge a picket of the enemy supposed to be at this place, but they found none. Marched thence across Beverly's ford on the Rappahannock & encamped this evening at Brandy Station, getting good feed for our horses. Found our wagons here & ordered to be ready to march tomorrow with 3 days rations. 2nd Va. Regiment reported here to Brigade for duty, in place of 9th Va. Regiment transferred to Gen. W.H.F. Lee's Brigade. Lt. John Loray & guide surprised & captured 3 Yankees early this morning. Rain close & steady to-day & night— ground very wet and the roads muddy & bad.

Nov. 21: Ordered to be ready to move at 10 a.m., but did not start till 1 p.m. Marched through Stephensburg & thence towards Ely's ford on the Rapidan—wagons went to

Germana Mills. Encamped tonight in Culpeper Co. 1¹/₂ miles from Ely's ford. Day clear.

Nov. 22: Moved at 8¹/₂ a.m. & crossed the Rapidan at Ely's ford, 15 miles from Fredericksburg. Came into Plank road at Chancellorsville in Spottsylvania & encamped on Telegraph Road on Mrs. Alsop's farm 5 miles from Fredericksburg. Wagons came up to-night. Met a number of citizens leaving Fredericksburg by order of the authorities from fear that the town might be shelled.

Nov. 23: Brigade moved up the river and encamped 8 miles from Fredericksburg near Barrow's ford. Clear & cool today.

Nov. 24: Changed camp today & encamped to-night near the track of the F'b'g & Orange R.R., 4th Regiment going on picket.

Nov. 25: Our Regiment went on picket today. I went to wagon camp to make out pay rolls for my former company. Rained hard tonight.

Nov. 26: Moved camp to Spottsylvania C.H. & camped in half a mile of the C.H. This county is very poor & scarce of forage.

Nov. 27: Clear & cool—Regiment still in camp at same place. Went to wagon camp & drew pay for my company & distributed it—also went to-night to Sanford's Tavern at Spottsylvania C.H. to assist Capt J.K. Jones in making out pay rolls for Sept. & Oct. and slept in bed. Though in bed, I spent a disagreeable night.

Nov. 28: In camp at same place & quiet.

Nov. 29: Quiet—nothing new.

Nov. 30: Went to church near the C.H. & heard Rev. Mr. Landstreet, of 1st Reg't, preach. Got orders to send 150 Men on picket tomorrow.

Dec. 1st: Took Capt. Chappell's & Capt. Field's squadrons on picket at W. States' & Banks' fords. Col. Owen remained with the balance of the Regiment & moved camp towards Mt. Pleasant. Received a dispatch tonight, while on picket, enjoining vigilance & stating that Gen. R.E. Lee had cause to believe enemy would make a move tomorrow.

Dec. 2: Visited Capt. Chappell's pickets today. Everything quiet.

Dec. 3: Visited Capt. Field's pickets today & went to Fredericksburg—found the town old looking & dilapidated. Pickets are confronting each other on the opposite banks of the river—Streets presented evidences of desertion. I saw Mrs. Washington's tombstone near the Paper mills in an unfinished state. Relieved by 4th Regiment late to-day & returned to camp on Mr. Cropp's farm, 3 miles from Mt. Pleasant.

Dec. 4: Still in camp.

Dec. 5: Snow two inches deep & everything quiet.

Dec. 6: Brigade moved today for convenience of forage & encamped on O.M. Crutchfield's farm. Weather overhead very pleasant, but roads muddy & bad.

Dec. 7: Day cold & clear. Quiet in camp.

Dec. 8: In camp—weather cold & clear.

Dec. 9: Still in camp.

Dec. 10: In camp & weather the same. Ordered to go on picket tomorrow with one squadron.

Dec. 11: Went on picket with Cap't Grey's squadron. Before day light the enemy opened on Fredericksburg with 148 heavy 20 pound parrott guns, with view of crossing—they crossed at Rail Road bridge & near the wire bridge, on pontoons, at 7 a.m. For a while they were repulsed, but finally succeeded in crossing. This evening Col. Owen with balance of the Regiment & Col. Wickham with the 4th came down to reinforce our picket & support it should the enemy attempt to cross. Camped near the forks of the road not far from Child's plantation.

Dec. 12: Enemy crossed in large numbers & Gen. R.E. Lee fell back, allowing him to occupy the town. Sharp skirmishing on the skirts of the town & heavy cannonading this evening—Loss not known on either side. Camped tonight at same place with everything quiet on our posts.

Dec. 13: Heavy fight today at Bernard's farm 2½ miles below Fredericksburg. General fight along the lines south of the town & enemy driven into town with heavy loss— say from 15,000 to 20,000 and 1626 prisoners. We lost about 4000 killed, captured & slightly wounded. Gens. Maxey Gregg of S.C. & T.R.R. Cobb of Ga. were killed today. Our Regiment with 4 pieces of artillery ordered to the Junction of the old turnpike & Plank roads, 5 miles from Fredericksburg. All quiet here to-day and to-night encamped in this place, being ordered to annoy enemy's right flank if occasion offered. Heavy fights tonight between one of our Brigades & the enemy on the edge of the town.

Dec. 14: Regiment remained still in same place. Artillery had a fight, but there was none of any consequence with small arms—general fight expected tomorrow. We hold our position & the enemy's dead.

Dec. 15: A beautiful day & Aurora Borealis last night. No fighting to-day of any moment save by artillery. I rode around our lines from plank road to Dr. Taylor's House on our extreme left. The enemy have batteries enfilading our line of batteries. Our army is confident & only asks that the enemy advance—Report tonight that Sigel is marching to cross the upper Rappahannock & Rapidan to turn our left, which report, however, proved groundless. Regiment still in same place with the artillery.

Dec. 16: Enemy evacuated Fredericksburg this morning, taking up or destroying their bridges behind them & retired behind the Stafford Hills. They left large numbers of their dead unburied & quantities of small arms on the field. They confess a terrible defeat. Brigade returned from Hamilton's crossing today. Our pickets were ordered to be strengthened & one piece of artillery was sent down—camped tonight near Haden's.

Dec. 17: Enemy still to-day & our army engaged in burying their own & the enemy's dead. Reported that Gens. Hill &

Jackson have gone down towards Port Royal, whither the enemy seem to be heading. Relieved today by portion of the 4th Regiment. It snowed & turned very cold late this evening & we camped near the track of Fredericksburg & Orange R.R.

Dec. 18: Moved to former camp on Crutchfield's farm & ordered to move to a place between Guinea's Station & Bowling Green.

Dec. 19: Moved camp to Caroline 3 miles from Guinea's Station. Clear & cold and nothing for horses to eat to-night.

Dec. 20: Still in camp.

Dec. 21: Moved camp today to Campbell's farm 3 miles from Guinea's Station towards Bowling Green.

Dec. 22: In camp still today. Col. Owen & myself qualified to our appointments as Lt. Col. & Major.

Dec. 23: In camp still. Cols. Drake, Munford, & Roper came to <u>head-quarters</u> of Regiment to examine Lt. Tynes as to his qualification for promotion to captaincy of Company "H." They found him incompetent & recommended that he be not promoted.

Dec. 24: Ordered on scout, myself, 192 men, 4 Capt's, & 8 Lieutenants & 5 days rations. Marched at 10^1/$_2$ a.m. & encamped for the night on F'b'g & Orange Plank road, one mile from Chancellorsville. Had rations of corn hauled to camp for us.

Dec. 25: Beautiful day. Left camp this morning at 10 o'clock & crossed the Rapidan at Ely's Ford, encamping one mile beyond in Culpeper Co. Gen. W.H.F. Lee's Brigade details of 800 men & 2 guns passed late this evening. Had a quiet Christmas.

Dec. 26: Marched at 3 a.m., the 3rd Regiment being in front, and crossed at Kelly's mill ford. Dismounted, remained here several hours, & fed on wheat straw. Marched through Morrisville & Elkton and encamped near Zoar Church in Fauquier Co. 15 miles from Warrenton & 20 from Dumfries.

Gen. Hampton came up today with his Brigade detail of 800 men & 2 guns. Detail of 45 men & 3 officers made from our Regiment for picket tonight—Good feed of hay for horses tonight.

Dec. 27: Marched this morning at 6½ o'clock, through Fauquier & a portion of Stafford & came into Telegraph road from Dumfries to Stafford C.H., 3 or 4 miles north of Acquia, 5th Regiment being in front. Marched towards Dumfries and captured 15 sutlers, 85 prisoners, 2 negroes & 8 or 10 wagons & teams with sutler's goods & c. Lt. W.S. Guy Company "E," on coming in with his picket this morning, charged & routed a party of the enemy who had placed themselves in his way to intercept him. Having charged vigorously, he & Lt. John Lamb, commanding another picket, came into the Regiment safely. Shelled Dumfries & opened on the enemy with sharpshooters, but they being 3000 or 4000 strong under Col. Caudy, we were unable to force them to evacuate the place. I was ordered by Gen. Stuart to hold the enemy in check, if they should advance from Acquia—at sunset was ordered to bring off the prisoners, artillery, & wagons and to go out on the Buntsville road. Being without a guide acquainted with the country & without definite instructions, added to the evils of <u>brandy</u> in the command, I found great difficulty in marching forward. Marched towards Buntsville & met a courier from Gen. Stuart, & late tonight met Cap't Smith of the 9th Regiment with orders for me to turn over to him the prisoners, horses, wagons, & artillery there without ammunition—all to be taken immediately to our rear through Fauquier. I had destroyed 2 wagons (sutler's), the teams being unable to pull them. Moved on & overtook the Brigade near Greenwood Church & encamped at 2 o'clock to-night. Cap't White being unable to get all the stragglers from the Brigade along, did not come up with the Regiment to-night.

Dec. 28: Moved out early this morning to meet an advance of the enemy, who attempted last night to take one of our pickets. While the 1st & 2nd Regiments charged the enemy in front, I was ordered with 5th Regiment in my rear to charge them on their flank as they were drawn up behind a house. They gave way and we pursued them killing, capturing & wounding about 150 or 175 of the 2nd & 17th Penn. Regiments of cavalry & 12th Illinois. They attempted to make a stand on the Fairfax side of the Occoquan, but gave way & we drove them to & from their camp on the road leading to Fairfax C.H. on Style's farm. The charge across the Occoquan by single file was the prettiest affair I ever witnessed. Col. Roper bolted at a house beyond the ford to collect the men, who had become very much scattered in the long charge & ordered me to lead the charge two miles further. I did so, driving them from their camp on Style's farm, capturing one wagon, several horses, & prisoners. In their fright a number of the enemy had run off into the bushes, leaving their horses picketed in the camp. Being but feebly supported, I fell back, reporting the fact to Gen. Lee who went with a large force, finding the camp abandoned, burnt it. The men got a number of overcoats, blankets, Buffalo robes, rubber clothes & commissaries from this camp. Corp'l M.J. Oliver company "E," was thrown from his horse & badly bruised while gallantly pursuing the enemy. Lt. A.H. Haskins, company K, & 20 men, being sent on the road towards Fairfax C.H., charged a party of the enemy on this road & captured 3 prisoners & a wagon & fine team. Marched towards Fairfax C.H. & crossed the rail road track at Burke's Station, tearing up the track & destroying some tents & capturing some prisoners. A small party under Gen. Lee struck off from this place & went very near Alexandria. Reaching the little river turnpike the division turned down towards Fairfax C.H. & on arriving in one mile of that place, the enemy's infantry in ambush opened on the head, of our column, fortunately killing only 2 horses & wounding one man very slightly. We made no reply to their fire & only withdrew out of musket range, where upon the enemy not knowing how to interpret it & thinking if might be a party of their own men, sent a flag of truce to ask whether we were friends or foes. They were told that they would be answered in the morning. On this being reported back, they began to shell the turnpike; but in the interim we had built camp fires, as if about to encamp for the night & had left, taking a cross road towards Vicuna. Private Geo. Nicholas, a substitute in company K, deserted tonight, but possessing no information as to our arrangements he was unable to do any harm. This was the only man lost today.

Dec. 29: Marched all last night—very cold & disagreeable— passing Vicuna on Alexandria, Loudon & Hampshire rail roads, Frying Pan in Fairfax county & stopped to feed at 10 a.m. at Chantilly. After resting here awhile, we came into a little river turnpike, crossed Cub river & encamped near Aldie tonight. Bought two days' rations for Regiment here & plenty of feed for horses. Had, altogether, a very pleasant time here. Had charge of the prisoners today.

Dec. 30: Moved at 12 M. today, passing through Middleburg & marching to "The Plain" on the Manassas Gap R.R. My Regiment encamped here for the night, while the action Regiments of the Brigade encamped 2 miles off. Placed the prisoners, for the night, in a church at this place. I took supper at Mr. Foster's & spent several hours very agreeably with the ladies at his house. Put out pickets on road to Warrenton, to Salem, & to Thoroughfare Gap.

Dec. 31: Moved early this morning at $7^1/2$ o'clock & marched to Culpeper C.H. by way of Hart's ford, below Waterloo bridge, Jeffersonton & Rixeyville, crossing the Hazel river at Rixey's ford. Hard march today for the prisoners & we reached Culpeper C.H. at $10^1/2$ P.M. & encamped on the east side, with corn for our horses to eat.

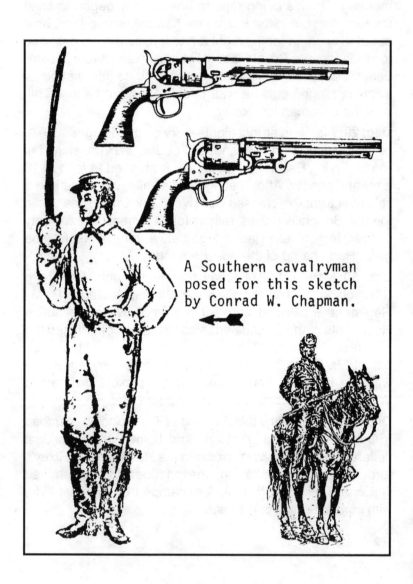

A Southern cavalryman posed for this sketch by Conrad W. Chapman.

1863

1863

Jan. 1st 1863: The new year opened beautifully—lovely day— and we closed our expedition with 2400 men & 6 pieces of artillery, with the loss of only 3 men wounded. One (Cap't Bullock of 5th Regt.) afterwards died of his wounds. Three hundred men were killed, wounded or captured by us. Sent the prisoners by railroad to Richmond. Heard that part of Siegel's army had crossed the Rappahannock & had come up to Ely's ford & Germanna's Mills on the Rapidan to intercept us. Marched at 8 a.m. & encamped in two miles of Chancellorsville.

Jan. 2: Marched to camp this evening & I found that Col. Owen had gone on leave of absence of 20 days from 25th of Dec.

Jan. 3: In camp still today. Distributed captured horses, saddles & arms.

Jan. 4: Everything quiet.

Jan. 5: Still in camp & had the novel occurrence of a lady to dine in my tent today. She came to look after her husband in the Regiment.

Jan. 6: In camp quiet & shoeing horses.

Jan. 7: Took the Regiment to field near Guinea's depot for Regimental inspection by Gen. Fitz Lee—they did tolerably well. Adjutant & myself went tonight to Brigade Hdquarters, on invitation, to attend a meeting of singers.

Jan. 8: Went on Brigade inspection & drill this morning to same field. To-night I paid a visit to Col. T.T. Munford of 2nd Regiment.

Jan. 9: Had Brigade review again before Gen. Fitz Lee at same place—Nothing else doing.

Jan. 10: Rainy & cold. Brigade went up near Fredericksburg to be reviewed by Gen. R.E. Lee—overcoats ordered to be taken off just before review, though it was cold & disagreeable. Quite an imposing affair! I went to see Gen. R.E. Lee & Gen. Stuart after the review, on business & had a very disagreeable trip back tonight in the rain.

Jan. 11: In camp quiet to-day & Chaplain McClelland preached. Sent in list of men without horses or with unserviceable ones.

Jan. 12: Brigade moved camp today at 9 a.m., marched through Bowling Green, Caroline Co., & took the road towards Hanover C.H. Encamped early this evening at Barke's Bridge on the Mattapony, 9 miles from Bowling Green.

Jan. 13: Encamped near Hebron Church in King William County. Very good camp, but water somewhat inconvenient.

Jan. 14: In camp quiet today & commenced drilling on horseback & foot. Adj't Dr. Grigg, S'gt Woodson, & myself were invited to Gen. Lee's Hdquarters tonight & had a pleasant time.

Jan. 15: Drilled twice today—Nothing new—Rained hard tonight.

Jan. 16: Drilled this evening.

Jan. 17: In camp still & commenced hearing recitations from the commissioned officers on tactics. Adj't heard <u>N.C.</u> noncommissioned officers.

Jan. 18: Pretty day remained in camp. Company inspection this morning & dress parade this evening.

Jan. 19th. Sent Capt. White with 60 men to Hanover Junct. to guard stores & do picket duty. Everything quiet—Drilled in squadron drills.

Jan. 20: In camp quiet, drilling as usual. Bowing, company "D.", was sent to Richmond to the Hospital sick with small pox.

Jan. 21: Rained last night & all today—no drill but remained in camp quiet.

Jan. 22: In camp. Rainy & bad day. Had recitations & no drill. Se'g't Garrett, company G., & 4 men were sent on picket to West Point to protect forage train below King Wm C.H.

Jan. 23: Capt's. Mathews & Field released from arrest today & Col. Owen returned to duty. Enemy threaten to cross at

Fredericksburg & our Brigade ordered to move towards Guiney's (depot) at 8 a.m.

Jan. 24: Marched this morning at 8 a.m. & encamped ¹/₄ of a mile this side of Bowling Green near D.C. Dejarnett's place. Left Cap't J.K. Jones in command of the camp. Cloudy day the roads muddy & bad.

Jan. 25: Marched today early & encamped near Guiney's on Mr. Washington's farm. Cap't Palmer borrowed corn of him for the command.

Jan. 26: Our generals are being satisfied that the enemy had declined attempting to cross at Fredericksburg, as they had not learned that Longstreet had not left with a portion of his army for the south. We marched today early for our old camp, arriving there at 4 ¹/₂ P.M. with both horses & men very tired.

Jan. 27: In camp today & it snowed and rained tonight. Ordered to attend Court Martial in Dyson's Case tomorrow at Massaponax.

Jan. 28: Started today in the snow for Massaponax. Had a very disagreeable ride & spent the night at Dr. Scott's in Caroline Co.

Jan. 29: Started at 10 a.m. & went to Mr. McAlley's in Spottsylvania—Clear today.

Jan. 30: Went to Massaponax today & found the Court Martial had adjourned to Hanover Junction to try Lt. Col. Pate of 5th Va. Cavalry & Lt. Ware of 5th Va. Cavalry, Lt. Guy, Lt. Palmore, & myself returned to Mr. McAlley's & spent the night. Roads very bad, rivers high, & weather clear.

Jan. 31: Marched to Mr. Wyatt's in Caroline & spent the night.

Feb. 1st. Day beautiful & pleasant—Returned to camp.

Feb. 2: In camp quiet. Col's. Munford of 2nd Reg., Drake of 1st with Col. Owen, convened at Hdquarters of 3rd Va. Cavalry to examine Capt Wm Collins' qualifications for Captaincy of Company H. They reported favorably to his appointment to that position. Heard glorious news of the naval victory off Charleston S.C. Snowed tonight.

Feb. 3: Very cold before day & the ground slightly covered with snow this morning. Everything quiet.

Feb. 4th. Nothing new. Went to see Gen. Fitz Lee to get permission to go to Richmond.

Feb. 5: Snowed today. I started very early to Richmond & arrived there at 3 P.M. after having a very disagreeable ride.

Feb. 6: Spent the day in Richmond, making arrangements to furnish myself with a suit of clothes. Bought very ordinary overcoat for $100 & contracted for uniform coat & pants to cost $180. Regiment in camp quiet.

Feb. 7: Came to Hanover C.H. on cars & rode thence to camp; found everything in statu quo.

Feb. 8: Beautiful day & most of the men went to church. Ordered to be ready to move tomorrow at 9 a.m. for Culpeper C.H. to relieve Gen. Hampton's Brigade.

Feb. 9: Started today at 9 a.m. & passing Chesterfield Depot on Rich'd & Fredericksburg R.R., encamped near Mt. Carmel Church in Caroline Co. Roads very muddy & cut up. A large number of men in the Regiment were sent home today to procure fresh horses.

Feb. 10: Moved at 8 a.m. & encamped near Waller's Tavern in Spottsylvania Co., the day being a beautiful one.

Feb. 11: Snowing & raining this morning & we moved at 8 a.m. & encamped near Vidersville, Orange co. Rainy & disagreeable night.

Feb. 12: Marched to Culpeper C.H., crossing the Rapidan at Somerville ford. Encamped in the East side of the village. Roads being very muddy & bad, the wagons did not come up tonight.

Feb. 13: Remained in camp near the C.H. all day. Wagons got up late tonight—beautiful day.

Feb. 14: Moved out & encamped one mile from the C.H. on Orange & Alexandria R.R. This camp was on Rev. Mr. George's place & a good one.

Feb. 15: Some of the men began to put chimney's to their tents. Sent out a squadron under Capt J.L. Jones on picket for 4 days, also sent 4 men on a scout to Warrenton, Fauquier co. Balance of the Regiment in camp quiet.

Feb. 16: Nothing new. Men busily fixing themselves.

Feb. 17: Snowed last night & to-day to depth of 6 inches. Col. Owen called Regimental Court Martial. Lt. W. Guy, Cap't R. H. Walkins & Cap't J.R. Christian to try cases in company D. for fighting.

Feb. 18th: Very bad & rainy day. No mail today, cars having broken down somewhere on the road. Col. Owen dissolved the Regimental court called yesterday, having dispersed of the cases otherwise.

Feb. 19: Pickets relieved today & Cap't J.R. Christian went out on picket. Several prisoners brought in, captured in Loudon & Fauquier Cos.

Feb. 20: In camp quiet. I went to Culpeper C.H. tonight to a concert of Brigade performers—a very fair success, Dr. J.R. Leigh returned to duty today.

Feb. 21: In camp quiet.

Feb. 22: Commenced snowing last night & a heavy storm today—snow 18 inches deep.

Feb. 23: Nothing new. I went to Culpeper C.H. today to make preparation to leave, by railroad on furlough of 20 days, Lt. J.H. Knight, after a long absence, returned to duty today. The enemy having withdrawn their cavalry and infantry pickets along the Rappahannock. Gen. Stuart ordered Gen. Fitz Lee to scout tomorrow to ascertain their whereabouts, intentions & c. I was ordered by Gen. Lee to take available portion of the Regiment on scout tomorrow at 8 a.m. without relieving the pickets.

Feb. 24: Col. Owen being sick, I deferred my departure on furlough & took Regiment on scout, having about 150 officers & men with 3 day's rations & as much corn as men could well carry on their horses. Marched at 9 a.m. through Culpeper

C.H. & Stevensburg and crossed the Rappahannock at Kelly's mill. On account of 18 inches snow roads were miserable & almost impassable. No ambulances with the command. Encamped near Morrisville Fauquier co. on Telegraph road from Warrenton. Got a plenty of hay for horses & notwithstanding the snow, the men spent a very agreeable night by scraping snow away & making beds with bushes & straw near large log fires. River so high as to swim low horses at the ford.

Feb. 25: Marched at 8 a.m. down Falmouth road, 1st Regiment being in front. On the march we passed Franklin gold mines & Hartwood church in Stafford county. Came upon enemy's pickets below Hartwood & charged them, 1st Regiment being in front & the 3rd in the rear. In the first charge the 1st Regiment & part of 2nd pursued the enemy to the left of Wallace's house on the "Poplar road". Balance of 2nd Regiment under Maj. Breckenridge, with the 3rd in reserve, pursued them down the Falmouth road. After charging several miles Gen. Lee had the rally sounded ordering the 1st & 2nd to form behind the 3rd. We had then pursued about a mile below Hammett's house & having captured a number of prisoners & accomplished our purpose, we began to retire by Echelon. The 2nd Regiment formed in line of battle at Hammetl's house & the 1st went to form in a field in their rear. Capt. Randolph of the Black Horse troop, having thrown out his company as sharpshooters to my front, I was ordered by Gen. Lee to withdraw & form behind the 1st Regiment. On moving back to obey this order I was met by several who were looking for Gen. Lee to inform him that a Regiment of Yankees was in the woods on the right of the road facing towards Falmouth. Moving up quickly to support Col. Drake of 1st Regiment, should the Regiment of Yankees, alleged to be in the woods near him attempt to charge him, I saw an officer on the right of road facing as aforesaid, waving his handkerchief to me. Learning from some stragglers that the party probably belonged to the enemy & thinking it merely a ruse for the purpose of disentangling the men from the woods, I threw the Regiment "left into line" to be ready to meet them in case they attempted to charge, & advanced myself to meet the flag of truce; whereupon Lt. Weth of 3rd Penn. cavalry surrendered himself & no men to me; 8 or 10 others came out and surrendered to Col. Drake of 1st Regiment. This proved to be the party supposed to be a Regiment of the enemy & I immediately informed Gen. Lee to that effect. While this was transpiring the enemy had advanced their sharpshooters within carbine range of Hammett's house & commenced firing on the 2nd Regiment, which was ordered to retire & form behind the 1st & 3rd stationed near Coakley's house. The enemy pressing, our sharpshooters were placed in the edge of the woods, 300 y'd's in advance of Coakley's house, on both sides of the road. In a very few minutes they drove in our sharpshooters & commenced following them up with a cheer, their skir-mishers being supported by a column in the road with drawn sabres. Gen. Lee ordered me to charge them with a yell, which the Regiment did in most gallant style, striking at the advancing column and disregarding the skirmishers on the flanks. They continued to move on till we came in 30 yards of them, when they broke & fled in perfect confusion. Pur-sued them ¼ of a mile, killing & capturing several, when thinking we had pursued as far as prudence would permit or was in accordance with the designs of Gen. Lee, we halted the column, formed it "front into line", & immediately received orders to return to the edge of the woods & form in line facing the enemy, which I did. Retiring from this position & coming in speaking distance of Gen. Lee, he highly complimented us for the gallant charge made, which com-pliment the men received with loud cheers. Enemy, after this charge, made no further effort to pursue & the prisoners were ordered across Kelly's ford. The detachment returned to same camp near Morrisville. Rain towards daybreak & very disagreeable. Our loss was 3 killed & 11 wounded & missing. The 3rd Regiment, though exposed to fire & met the enemy coming to charge us, fortunately lost none. Lt.

C.R. Palmare, Company G., acting assistant surgeon, was left in the enemy's lines to care for the wounded whom it was impossible to bring off as we had no ambulances. Loss of the enemy must have been 200; 145 men & 5 officers, representing several different Regiments, were brought as prisoners to Richmond.

Feb. 26: Moved out at 8 a.m. & returned to camp, the 3rd Regiment being in the rear.

Feb. 27: Prisoners were sent to Richmond on cars in charge of Lt. Ryals. Went home by cars on furlough for 20 days— Regiment in camp quiet. I found 5th Reg. at Orange C.H. on its way to join the Brigade.

Feb. 28: In camp quiet. Horses have had no corn for 4 days.

March 1st. Clear & windy. 4th Regiment came up from Spottsylvania, where they had been for a long time on picket, & encamped near us. Horses got half rations of corn today & pickets were relieved.

Mch. 2: Warm & pleasant—nothing new.

Mc'h. 3: Weather changeable—Everything quiet.

Mch. 4: In camp quiet.

Mc'h 5: Windy. Company A under Capt. White having been left at Hanover Junction, came up today.

Mc'h 6: Rain & hail before daybreak. Pickets relieved.

Mc'h 7: Hard rain during the night. In camp quiet.

Mc'h 8: Capt. John S. Mosby with 30 men made a raid on the enemy's lines at Fairfax C.H., capturing Brig. Gen. Stoughton, 2 captains, & 33 privates, surprising them in their beds. He took a number of horses also & brought the whole off without any loss.

Mc'h 9: Col. Owen reported all the horses in the Regiment that were unfit for duty from want of forage.

Mc'h 10: Cold & disagreeable rain. Gen. Lee sent L't Ryals & others to inspect the horses of Regiment reported unfit for duty. They returned 101 as unserviceable; the rest, they thought, could do duty on two feeds of grain.

Mc'h 11: Weather threatening. Adj't McClellan went to Richmond in charge of prisoners captured by Capt Mosby.

Mc'h 12: In camp quiet.

Mc'h 13: Pleasant day, Gen. Lee ordered 2 new posts to be established at Brownings & Sycamore fords on the Hazel river.

Mc'h 14: Cloudy & windy. In camp quiet.

Mch 15: Cold & cloudy. Rumors of an advance of the enemy—several thousand reported near Loa Church in Fauquier.

Mc'h 16: Cold wind & some rain in afternoon. Three thousand Yankee cavalry & artillery reported near Kelly's ford, and a circular sent to the Regiments to have all their sharpshooters out at daybreak & to send them down the railroad to the road leading from Brandy Station to Kelly's ford; then to wait for orders, Regiments holding themselves ready to move at a moment's warning.

Mc'h 17: Boots & saddles sounded at 7 a.m. & Regiment soon on the road to Kelly's ford via Brandy Station, 3rd squadron, under Cap't Chappell, being in front & 1st under Cap't Field in the rear. Moved at a brisk trot as far as Miller's house & here formed in order of battle, 1½ miles below Brandy Station. Col. Owen called around his company commanders & asked them to do their duty & to see that their men did the same. Remaining here a few moments the Brigade moved off down the road at a brisk gallop; the 3rd Regiment being in front preceded by the sharpshooters. Soon came in sight of the enemy with their right wing resting on the river at Wheatley's ford & their left extending a short distance beyond Brook's house. They had a large number of dismounted sharpshooters posted behind a stone fence connecting these two places & a heavy mounted reserve drawn up in the fields & woods, on both sides of the road, branching off from Wheatley's to Kelly's ford. Our sharpshooters were soon engaged with theirs, and throwing down the fence about 100 yards below Brandon's house, the Regiment came into the field & fell back to Brown's house

& in Wheatley's field to form. Here all were met by Gen. Lee, who ordered Col. Owen to charge the enemy. This was done in gallant style, Regiment sweeping down the fence along the road & passing through an opening between the rail fence, running at right angles across the field from Brook's house, and the rock fence. We found it impossible to get through the stone fence to them & so the Regiment turned across the field to our left, to some straw stacks & wheeled down towards Wheatley's ice house, hoping to be able to get at their right flank. But observing this, the enemy's sharp-shooters, who had fled from the approach of the column, returned to their posts & poured a hot fire into it as it passed & crowded into Wheatley's houses & garden. Several of our number were wounded. On our left was the 5th Regiment, under Col. Roper, advancing to charge enemy's right flank & the 3rd advancing to their support. But getting to the house of G.T. Wheatley, they were unable to advance because of obstructions placed in the outlet by the enemy. Blocked up here all remained a considerable time under a galling fire from the enemy posted in & around Wheatley's houses at a range of not more than 75 yd's. Here S'g't G.M. Betts, com-pany C., fell, and moving out from this position a few hun-dred yards, Maj. Puller of the 5th Regiment was killed. The 1st, 2nd & 4th Regiments charged the enemy as they ad-vanced through Wheatley's field from behind the stone wall. Here Maj. Breckenridge of the 2nd was captured—this was the first charge. We moved through Weatley's field into a field of Miss Wheatley (place occupied by Lampkin) & the 3rd charged again through the triangular lot in front of Lampkin's house. But owing to the narrowness of the gate & the confusion produced by the 5th attempting to pass out at the same time, not more than 15 or 20 men followed the Col. into the lot, who charged up to within 50 y'd's of the fence on the west of Wheatley's field. Finding it impossible to dislodge the enemy's sharpshooters from behind the fence, this party retired through another gate by Lampkin's stable. The enemy's fire was concentrated upon these gates

& they wounded several & killed J.T. Wilkins, company C, & W.W. Young, company B at this place. Maj. Pelham of the artillery fell in this field, shot in the head by a shell. This was the second charge.

Retiring from this charge we moved over on the main road leading from Brandy Station to Kelly's ford & formed a line of battle near Caster's run on the farm of Jas. Newby. The 1st, 5th & 3rd Regiments charged on the left of the road facing towards Kellysville; while 2nd & 4th charged on the opposite side, making a line of the entire Brigade. The enemy formed in the edge of the woods opposite & advanced with the sharpshooters across the field & with a battery of 3 guns in Brown's field; they were gallantly met by our sharpshooters & our Brigade remained some time exposed to a galling fire from the enemy's sharpshooters before they were ordered to charge. Presently our artillery opened upon them & soon the order came for a simultaneous charge of the whole Brigade, commencing on the right. The 3rd commenced the charge by fours, and advancing 300 yards, were fronted into line & ordered to charge in line; but owing to the inequality of the ground, this was found impracticable & they were again ordered to charge by fours. A battery of 3 of the enemy's guns was playing on us from the moment we commenced the charge. Some of the men passed several hundred y'd's beyond the Battery, causing the most of the gunners to desert their pieces, & were only prevented from capturing the guns by a double fence which intervened & a heavy line of sharpshooters posted in the edge of the woods & behind the fences. Finding no impression could be made upon the enemy, we fell back to Caster's Run the point at which the charge was commenced & reformed, the enemy not daring to follow us into the open fields. Ordered back on the road to within 2 miles of Brandy Station. Here we remained till about sunset; then ordered to follow the enemy on his retreat across the river. Marched to ½ mile of Kelly's ford & hearing that the whole force had recrossed the river, we returned to the same camp at 12 P.M. This was the heaviest

Beverly Ford

Kelly's Ford

**"Fleetwood Hill," where most of the fighting
took place at the Battle of Brandy Station**

The Editor

loss that our cavalry have sustained in a fight during the war. It was as follows:

	Killed	Wounded	Missing		Total
1st Regiment	1	7	0	=	8
2nd "	1	18	15	=	34
3rd "	4	37	3	=	44
4th "	2	17	16	=	35
5th "	2	9	0	=	11
Maj Pelham Killed	1			=	1
					133

Many of these were very slightly wounded. Those in the 3rd Regiment who were sufficiently wounded to go to Hospital & the killed are as follows: Company A.—Private J.E. Reynolds wounded seriously. Company B.—W.W. Young killed; L't G.C. Mellen, J.B. Herbert & private A.W. West wounded. Company C.—S'g't G.M. Betts & private J.T.

Wilkins killed; Lt Jas. W. Hall wounded very seriously. Company D.—Privates Jas. E. Adams, L.A. Marston & F. Mountcastle wounded. Company E.—Corpl. Jno. R. Foster wounded in the arm. Company F.—L't B.W. Lacy & Se'g't Apperson wounded. Company G.—Private J.W. Bryant, H.F. Goodman wounded & private I.S. Fowler killed. Company H.—L't Jas. V. Garner, Private Jas. Green, E. Cage & Thos. Walker wounded. Company I.—Corp'l. A.A. Dance wounded. Company K.—Private Henry W. Edmonds, J.R. Cuningham, L. Scott, & C.A. Bondurant wounded. Thus ended this day. While the loss on our side was heavy, in men & horses, the enemy, in attempting to cross the river, lost more in killed than our own; and which we had to mourn the loss of some of our best men, are succeeded in preventing the enemy from accomplishing their purpose of making a raid through the country & destroying the rail road Bridge across the Rapidan. Our men with vastly inferior numbers & with horses which had not been fed in some time, held the insolent foe in check.

No feed tonight for horses or men. Wagons left for Orange C.H. at 10 a.m.

Mc'h 18: Remained in same place & this evening got some corn for our horses. Wounded treated at Brandy Station & sent off to Gordonsville.

Mc'h 19: Wagons returned from Orange C.H. today. Lt C.R. Palmore & myself came up to Regiment today.

Mc'h. 20: Commenced snowing. In camp quiet.

Mc'h 21: Snowing all day & rain tonight. Pickets relieved & the 7 Yankee officers, captured by Capt. Mosby near Drainsville, were sent to Richmond today. He also captured 21 privates at same time, whom he paroled & released.

Mc'h 22: Sun came out today & nearly all the snow has melted—warm & pleasant. Had dress parade this evening.

Mc'h 23: Nothing new. I & others went down to the Battlefield & rode over it. Ordered to send to Albemarle for our wagons preparatory to moving.

Mc'h 24: Rainy & disagreeable day with hard rain all night.

Mc'h 25: In camp quiet & weather changeable.

Mc'h 26: Pickets relieved today & dress parade this evening. Thirty seven Yankee privates & one officer, taken by Capt Mosby, were brought in. Orders read this evening to observe tomorrow as a day of fasting & prayer & chaplains to perform services in all the Regiments.

Mc'h 27: Beautiful day, Rev. Mr. Meredith, chaplain of 4th Regiment preached for us today at 3$^1/_2$ P.M. In command of Regiment myself as Col. Owen went to Gordonsville today. Rain tonight.

Mc'h. 28: In camp quiet.

Mc'h 29: Beautiful day & nothing new.

Mc'h 30: Went to C.H. today as a witness in private R. Dyson's case. Capt Walkins, company K. returned today. Snowed late tonight.

Mc'h 31: Snowed till 10 a.m. then cleared off.

Ap'l 1st: Clear & cold. Cap't F. Guy offered his resignation today, on score of disability.

Ap'l. 2: Beautiful day. Regiments of the Brigade reviewed & inspected by L't Col. Tyler. Details for me to get fresh horses came in today.

Ap'l. 3: Clear & pleasant. Cap't Mosby sent in 18 prisoners captured near Drainsville. He killed about 25 & they left 15 wounded on the field. They partially surprised him, but by the courage of his men he drove them back, killing & capturing the above numbers. He had 60 men with him.

Ap'l 4: Windy & cold. Received order enquiring how much transportation we have & what it is. Snow tonight 5 inches deep.

Ap'l 5th: In camp quiet. Sent a Yankee Lieutenant, who was badly wounded in the fight of the 17th, across Kelly's ford to his friends, under a flag of truce.

Apl. 6: Nothing new & rain tonight.

Apl. 7: I went with Cap't Irving of 1st Regiment & Corp'l Jas. H. Allen of 6th Regiment to Kelly's ford to examine the locality with reference to a court of Enquiry as to defence of said ford. Regiment had a sabre drill today.

Apl. 8: Beautiful day. Drilled this morning in squadron drill.

Apl. 9: Sent off all surplus baggage & part of tents, preparatory to moving.

Apl. 10: Relieved pickets today & received orders to move tomorrow at 9 a.m.—4th Regiment started this morning.

Apl. 11: Brigade started today at 9 a.m.; crossing the Hazel river at Starke's ford, passing Jeffersonton, & encamping for the night beyond Amisville, Rappahannock Co. ¹/₂ mile.

Ap'l 12: Moved at 8 a.m., crossed the Rappahannock at Hinsons Mill, passed Orleans, & encamped on Rixey's farm in 3¹/₂ miles of Salem. Wagons came up & tents were pitched. Rain tonight.

Apl. 13th: In camp quiet. Gen. Fitz Lee came up today from Culpeper C.H. & 2 Yankee prisoners, brought in by Capt Mosby, were sent to this Regiment to be guarded. Day clear.

Ap'l 14: Started to move camp nearer to Salem on Manassas Gap R.R., but Learning that a large force of Yankee cavalry was at Morrisville, preparatory to attempting a crossing at Kelly's and attacking Gen. W.H.F. Lee's force, we were ordered to move back to Amisville, where we encamped for the night. Enemy made several attempts to cross at Rappahannock R.R. Bridge & at Kelly's. They crossed one squadron at Rappahannock bridge, which retired across the river as soon as our men approached. Lt Col. Payne of 4th Regiment, in reconnoitering, had a fight with the enemy near Warrenton, but meeting with a superior force, he had 2 killed & several wounded. Rain late night.

Apl. 15: Rainy & cold all day. Ordered to start for Culpeper C.H., but having marched two miles, the orders were countermanded & we returned to the same camp. With no dry place to pitch a tent had a very disagreeable night. The enemy made an effort again today to cross and succeeded at

Welford's, bearing down to Beverley's ford with a Regiment. They were charged by Gen. W.H.F. Lee's Brigade & 30 of them were captured and a number drowned in their effort to recross the river, which was much swollen from the rains.

Apl. 16: Marched this morning to Sperryville via Gaines' Cross-roads & Little Washington and encamped in 1¼ miles of Sperryville, Rappahannock Co. Cap't Christian, company F. brought up a Yankee Lieut. Captured by the Black Horse company this evening. Day clear & pleasant.

Apl. 17: In camp quiet. Picketing towards Gaines' X roads.

Apl. 18: Nothing new. Drilled this evening in squadron drill & sent out Cap't Field's squadron on picket beyond Little Washington.

Apl. 19: Pretty day & in camp quiet. The artillery started this evening for Culpeper C.H. via Guffriesburg.

Apl. 20: Moved at 6 a.m. for Culpeper C.H., passing by Sperryville, a beautiful mountain town on the turnpike leading from Warrenton through Thornton's Gap. Passed Woodville & Guffriesburg & encamped in one mile of the C.H. on the Rixeyville road. The Nottoway boys came up bringing me a new horse. Myself in command of Regiment, Col. Owen being sick.

Ap'l 21: In camp quiet & uncomfortable, there being but little wood.

Apl. 22: In camp quiet & the day pretty.

Apl 23: Sent out Cap't Mathew's squadron on picket. Rainy & disagreeable day.

Apl. 24: In camp & rain nearly all day.

Apl. 25: Had Brigade inspection today in line & dress parade in regular style, on foot, this evening. Officers & non-commissioned officers being unacquainted, the ceremony was gone through with somewhat awkwardly. Our pickets relieved today by another Regiment.

Apl. 26: Beautiful day & we moved camp one mile to Rev. Mr. George's place on the road to Brandy Station.

Apl. 27: 2nd & 4th Regiments moved camp today & the baggage was sent off to Gordonsville.

Apl. 28: In camp quiet.

Apl. 29: Received orders to send the wagons with baggage to the rear at 4½ a.m.—to Orange C.H. & to prepare the Regiment to mount. The wagons moved off at 5½ a.m. & at 6 the Regiment started out towards Brandy Station, with the balance of the Brigade, to meet the enemy, who had crossed during the night at Kelly's ford. The different Regiments dismounted at Brandy for some time &, ascertaining that the enemy were moving out towards Madden's, Brigade moved over on the road leading from Stevensburg to Madden's. Sending forward sharpshooters, 50 or 60 Yankees were captured & the road along which they were passing, was shelled for some time. After dark we sent back a detail for corn and rations to Culpeper C.H., while the Brigade moved across the Rapidan at Raccoon ford. In the darkness of the night the Regiment became separated. The portion with Col. Owen camped near Locust Grove in Orange Co., myself & a few others, being unable to find the Regiment, encamped at a little farm house in 3 miles of Locust Grove.

Apl. 30: This morning I collected the larger portion of the Regiment & remained with the Brigade. That portion under Col. Owen made an effort to get between the enemy & Fredericksburg, but finding them ahead of him at Chancellorsville, he turned off south of the Plank road & went around them by way of Todd's Tavern. The Brigade remained on the turnpike below Locust Grove for some time, shelling the enemy & with sharpshooters deployed, these moved out on the Plank road & finding the Brook road open, marched towards Spottsylvania C.H. via Todd's Tavern. Hearing here that the enemy's cavalry had gotten ahead of us on this road, the 5th Regiment, (commanded by Lt Col. Tyler) being in front, was ordered up the road to charge them, if necessary; while I was ordered to follow on, at a walk to support him. The 5th Regiment came up with the enemy at

Hugh Alsop's gate & charged them, while the enemy closed the road behind them as soon as they passed up. Pursuing with drawn sabres, at a brisk trot to Col. Tyler's support, we fell in with the enemy at the forks of two roads a half mile below Alsop's gate. Finding they were the enemy, I ordered the Regiment to charge, whereupon the enemy fled in every direction through the woods. Fearing a collision with the 5th Regiment, as it was quite dark & I had heard nothing from two couriers sent to inform Col. Tyler that I was moving to his support & besides not knowing which fork they had taken, I halted here to wait further developments and moved back the Regiment 100 yards below the forks of the road. Presently there was another advance & we killed 10 & wounded a number, among whom was their Lt Col. & 2 Capts. Soon a cry arose that we were shooting our friends & finding some of the 5th Regiment mixed up among us, I ordered the men to cease firing. This was done & we moved back slowly down the road to ascertain if we were mistaken & to prevent a flank movement from a road leading off in the direction of the enemy. The 2nd Regiment then charged up the road & captured 12 of a picket which they had again placed in the road after all retired. I had one man, private M. Blackstack of company H., badly wounded in the hand & I had my horse shot in the shoulder. Several of the men got separated in the dark & several were captured by the enemy, but got away from them & came up next day. We killed 10 & wounded a number—captured 2 horses, 2 prisoners & some arms. But for the darkness & fear that we were firing upon our own men (5th Reg.) we could have killed or captured the whole party. Encamped late tonight at Spottsylvania Court House.

May 1st. Nothing to feed our horses on. Marched back this morning nearly to Todd's tavern & ordered to return & go towards Fredericksburg by way of the Furnace. Our forces had a fight with the enemy near this place & drove in this right wing. After passing through a bye road to open communication with Gen. Fitz Lee, who, with the 2nd & 5th Regiments,

was on the Brock road, we returned & encamped late tonight at the Furnace. Corn detail came up & brought the first
feed we have had for two days. Maj. R.C. Price was killed
near this place today. Part of the Regiment with Col. Owen,
supported by 2 companies of Infantry, moved out on the
road to reconnoitre & ascertain about the advance of the
enemy down the river towards Banks' ford. They captured a
Yankee major today.

May 2nd. Ordered early this morning to support the artillery
of Gen. Stuart; but Gen. Jackson's command passing the
Furnace, we were ordered to return to Furnace and vidette
the right flank of our army as they passed. About 11 a.m. or
12 a.m. the enemy discovered the column moving & commenced shelling the road & advancing his sharpshooters
for the purpose of breaking our lines at this point. Just as
the rear of Gen. A.P. Hill's command had passed, they made
a desperate effort to capture his ordnance train. They forced
back the 22nd Ga. (Infantry) Regiment & I immediately ap-
plied to Col. Brown for a couple of pieces of artillery, which
he furnished. They were run up to the Furnace, fired, and
brought off; thus gaining the necessary time to get off the
train. I had also sent to the nearest Infantry commanders for
troops & Gen. Archer with his Brigade returned. Gen. Archer failing to call in the Infantry which had been placed in
the railroad cut, when he retired, I took the responsibility of
calling them in myself & thus saved them all except 2 companies, to whom the enemy had approached too near to
permit their getting out of the cut. They surrendered to the
enemy. Brought up the rear of Jackson's army & camped
for the night on the Plank road, near the wilderness church,
with nothing for horses or men to eat except some nice beef
captured from the enemy. Lt B. Hill Carter, company D, was
wounded yesterday near Loar Church on the turnpike & died
today. Part of the Regiment with Col. Owen was ordered today to unite with & co-operate with Col. W. Chappell's squadron picketed towards the house of Mr. Child's. Gen. Jackson
was wounded tonight by his own men, through mistake. Gen.

CHANCELLORSVILLE · Evening
Jackson's March, May 2, 1863
+ Spot where Jackson fell

Clifford Dowdey

Sedgwick crossed at or near Fredericksburg today & was met by Gen. Barksdale.

May. 3: Beautiful day & terrific fighting along the Plank road from the Wilderness to Chancellorsville. Woods set on fire by shells, causing many wounded men to die. Enemy driven north of the Plank road. We moved out early today & remained, near Chancellor's house, dismounted for several hours. Then ordered to follow the first Regiment down the road, leading into the one from the Plank road to Ely's ford, to see if there were any of enemy on said road. Finding it strongly guarded, we returned & took another road, arriving into said road ½ mile from Ely's ford. We captured several of the rear guard of Averall's Division of cavalry, which had just passed up towards Chancellorsville. After opening this road & scouting to Ely's ford, we left pickets at the ford & where we went into the Ely's ford road & then camped in the woods with nothing for men or horses to eat. Part of the Regiment with Col. Owen picketed towards Child's House on the road leading towards U. States ford. Heights of Fredericksburg recaptured tonight.

May 4: Fight not very heavy today. Ordered to Spottsylvania C.H. to relieve 2nd N.C. Cavalry. Yankee Cavalry under Stoneman reported to be doing heavy damage at Louisa C.H. & other places. Put out pickets at Todds tavern, but did not relieve Lt. Col. Payne this evening. Gen. Sedgewick succeeded in recrossing the river at Banks' ford after being nearly surrounded.

May 5: Relieved the pickets of 2nd N.C. this morning. Enemy under Stoneman reported as returning by this route in heavy force. Wagons were hitched up preparatory to falling back to Todd's tavern, but report proving groundless, the wagons returned to same camp. Rain this evening & train came through from Richmond to Guiney's today. Hookers army recrossed the river at U. States ford tonight. Our army in no condition for pursuit & no effort was made to do anything further than pick up stragglers.

May 6: Rainy & disagreeable & still at Spottsylvania C.H. picketing. Had the horses, belonging to the different Regiments in Brigade, examined & those in very bad condition were sent to pasture near the C.H. Part of the Regiment with Col. Owen spent the day picking up stragglers in the woods between Chancellorsville & U. States ford, and encamped tonight near Todd's tavern.

May 7: Still at Spottsylvania C.H. Received orders to call in the pickets & follow on after the Brigade, along Plank road to Orange C.H., which Brigade was making an effort to intercept Stoneman. Left the sick in charge of Dr. Randolph of 1st Va. Cavalry at this place; detailed 4 men to report to Dr. Fontaine to proceed to Beaver dam & along the line of the Central R.R. & ascertain the damage Stoneman had done to the R.R. Stoneman's cavalry passed Vidiersville today on his return from the raid.

May 8: Started at 1 a.m. & marched till 11 a.m. when we overtook the balance of the Regiment near Orange C.H. Roads very muddy & march disagreeable. Captured some stragglers from Stoneman's command. Encamped on Lewis R. William's place, one mile from the C.H., with plenty of feed for horses, but nothing for men.

May 9: Beautiful day, appointed by Gen. R.E. Lee as a day of Thanksgiving & prayer for our great victory. Mr. McClelland preached in the camp this evening.

May 11: In camp quiet & sent out two scouting parties to ascertain if any enemy were in Culpeper County.

May 12: Nothing new. The detachment left near Spottsylvania C.H. to graze horses came up this evening.

May 13: In camp quiet. The scouts, sent to Culpeper, returned reporting no Yankees south of the Rappahannock.

May 14: Nothing new.

May 15: Regiment reviewed & inspected by Lt G.M. Ryals— Brigade inspection this evening. Hood's division moved near Raccoon ford today.

May 16: Moved at 6 a.m. across Halladay's ford at Rapidan Station to Culpeper C.H. & encamped on Mr. George's place in same spot. We have now 3 Brigades near the C.H. for duty; viz, Brig. Gen. Fitz Lee's, Brig. Gen. W.H.F. Lee's, & Brig. Gen. Wade Hampton's.

May 17: Beautiful day & Rev. Mr. Cole from Culpeper C.H. preached to the Regiment this evening at 4 o'clock.

May 18: 2nd Regiment came up from Vidiersville yesterday & Cap't Chappell's squadron went on picket for 4 days. Received orders to organize all dismounted men into a Battalion to be armed with rifles.

May 19: In camp quiet & Cap't Mosby sent up 4 prisoners taken near Dumfries today.

May 20: In camp quiet.

May 21: Had Brigade review & drill today of 4 Regiments, in Mr. Bradford's field.

May 22: Gen. Stuart with Maj. Gen. Hood & Mr. Wigfall, senator from Texas, reviewed the 3 Brigades (Fitz Lee's, W.H.F. Lee's & Wade Hampton's) that were present, in a large field near Brandy Station—5000 men mounted & the most magnificent sight I ever witnessed. A Beautiful day & quite a large turnout of the ladies, considering the times.

May 23: Very warm day & every thing quiet.

May 24: Rev. Mr. Cole preached to the Regiment this evening. Regiment kept in the camp & considered on duty as grand guard.

May 25: Had regimental drill today & Maj. McClellan came over from Gen. Stuart's Hdquarters to inspect the books of the Regiment.

May 26: In camp quiet. Ten men of the Regiment sent, on foot, across the Rappahannock & armed with Austrian rifles to supply themselves with horses from the enemy.

May 27: Quiet; had dress parade this eve.

May 28: On grand guard today & had election in camp for state officers. For Gov. Thos. S. Flournay 167 votes; Wm. Smith 109; G.W. Munford 12 votes.

May 29: Had Regimental drill today.

May 30: Every thing quiet.

May 31: Preaching in camp by Rev. Mr. George this morning & again this evening by Rev. Mr. Carson of Culpeper Co. Several ladies were in attendance—a rare sight in camp.

June 1st: In camp quiet.

June 2: Drilled in the regimental drill. Some rain tonight.

June 3: Col. Owen, with a detail of 300 men from different Regiments, was ordered to scout from the Furnace to Waterloo ford. At Warrenton Springs seeing a small picket of enemy on the opposite hill near the road towards Bealeton Station, he sent a part of Capt Field's squadron to charge & capture them, if possible. The enemy seeing our force from the hill, stood their ground & wounded with the sabre as follows: Private R.T. Jelen & R. Dyson company E.; W.H. Terrell company F.; F.A. Jones, M.P. Wells & G.W. Skinner company I. Three of the enemy were killed & two captured. Col. Owen advancing with the rest of his force, the enemy retreated and he then returned to Oak Shade & went into camp, leaving pickets at the various fords on the Rappahannock, with instructions to come in at daybreak tomorrow. Rev. Mr. George preached in camp tonight.

June 4: Col. Owen returned to camp this morning leaving Field's squadron on picket along the Hazel. Gen. Hood came up to Culpeper C.H. with his Division this evening. Had a regimental court for Capts. Matthews, White & Lt J.H. Knight to try private Skelly, company K., on charge of drunkeness & absence from camp without a leave in writing. They found him not guilty & acquitted him, the testimony being insufficient to convict him.

June 5: Grand review of 5 Brigades; viz, Fitz Lee's, W.H.F. Lee's & Hampton's, Robertson's & Jones—today in field near Brandy Station. A fine & very imposing affair—8000 men mounted—and Hood's division was present to witness it. Enemy reported to be crossing the Rappahannock at Warrenton Springs. Sent out a party to strengthen the picket at Rixey's ford, if necessary.

June 6: Started at 4¹/₂ P.M. with 3 days rations & moved across Wellford's ford on the Hazel, encamping, after dark, in a few hundred yards of the ford after crossing. The wagons encamped on Wellford's farm on the south side of the river. Col. Munford in command of the Brigade and Private G. Crofton, having crossed the river to get something to eat, was captured by the enemy.

June 7: Moved at 7 a.m. & recrossed the river & turning up, crossed again at Starke's ford & remained in a field near Oak Shade Church grazing all day. Encamped in the wood at this point tonight, wagons coming up at 9 P.M. 1st Regiment on picket from Hinson's ford to Waterloo bridge.

June 8: At 9 a.m. the 2nd & 3rd Regiments marched to field near Brandy Station & were reviewed by Gen. R.E. Lee, Gens. Ewell, Longstreet & c. being present & parts of same Brigades as on 5th instant. After the review we returned to same camp near Oakshade. Se'g't Wm. Lee, company B, & Ryan, company A, came in, having been sent out to get horses—they brought one prisoner. The party of dismounted men sent out to get horses, succeeded in getting two animals, which were brought off by members of 1st Reg.

June 9: Enemy crossed the Rappahannock at Beverly's & Kelly's fords at day this morning, driving in Gen. Jones' pickets. They advanced in heavy force with Infantry, artillery, & cavalry. The 1st, 2nd & 3rd Regiments moved across Starke's ford & thence towards Wellford's ford about 11 a.m. Finding the enemy in Wellford's field, we turned to the south of the road & moved down towards Beverly's, coming upon the enemy in one mile of Wellford's towards Brandy Station. Our sharpshooters advanced & were deployed in line, driving them back towards Beverly's ford. Here we remained some time moving right & left. This was the heaviest most extensive cavalry fight of the war in Va. up to this time; the enemy having 2 divisions of cavalry & a force of Infantry and we one division of cavalry. Loss in our Brigade as follows:

Battle of Brandy Station

In this action more than 20,000 Blue and Gray troopers crossed sabres in the greatest cavalry battle ever fought in the Western Hemisphere. The Union forces included 3,000 infantrymen and artillery support.

F. Downey

	Killed	Wounded	Missing	Total
1st Reg.	0	2	0	2
2nd "	2	8	0	10
3rd "	1	7	0	8
4th "	0	25	27	52
5th " on picket & not in the fight				
Grand total	3	42	27	= 72

Loss in the Division was 50 killed, 280 wounded & 130 missing = total 450.

In 3rd Regiment Se'g't R.H. Simmons, company A, was killed; Lt. J.P. Puryear, company A., shot through both legs. Priv. W.H. Smith company A., F.W. Guy, company E.; Chas. Carter company D.; R.I. Eggleston company D. all wounded. Enemy's loss was from 600 to 800 as far as could be ascertained. Enemy having retired across the river, we returned to same camp at Oakshade Church, putting out pickets towards Fox's & Freeman's fords.

June 10: In camp quiet today. 4th Regiment came up & joined the Brigade.

June 11: Quiet & Lt G.M. Ryals inspected the Regiment this evening.

June 12: In camp quiet & weather very dry.

June 13: At 12 M. ordered to mount & move out towards Jeffersonton, as enemy were reported to be crossing the Rappahannock at or below the Springs. Went in $1/2$ mile of Jeffersonton & finding the report false, returned to camp.

June 14: This evening we moved out by Amisville to Gaines' X roads & had a very good camp here. Firing reported to be heard in the direction of Winchester & enemy have crossed the Rappahannock at Waterloo bridge & Miller's factory.

June 15: Changed camp this morning & went on road towards Orleans $1/2$ mile from Gaines' X roads. Four prisoners were sent to be guarded & will be sent to Culpeper C.H. tomorrow.

June 16: Sent Cap't Mathew's squadron on picket from Warrenton Springs to Hinson's Mill and the balance of the Regiment moved out at 7 a.m., crossing the Rappahannock at Rock ford. Marched to Barker's X roads & thence to Marham; remained here dismounted several hours & then marched towards Paris, encamping at Somerset Mills in Fauquier.

June 17: Moved to Upperville, leaving Paris to our left; thence to Middleburg & turned to left of Aldie on the turnpike to Snicker's gap, to get some corn. While 2nd & 3rd Regiments were feeding, the enemy advanced rapidly on Aldie. We mounted & moved out hurriedly on the pike & found the 4th & 5th Regiments falling back on the Snickersville pike. Col. Munford, commanding the Brigade having determined to attempt to drive back the enemy, the 3rd was ordered to charge down the road & the 2nd & 4th to charge their flanks as this was done in gallant style. Following another charge we were forced to retire. A larger number of the enemy were killed & wounded than I have known in a cavalry fight of the same duration. The 5th Regiment made several charges before the 2nd & 3rd had gotten on the field. The 1st being with the artillery on the turnpike to Middleburg, was not much engaged. Loss in Brigade as follows.

	Killed		Wounded		Missing		Total
1st Reg.	0		5		1		6
2nd "	0		17		8		25
3rd "	0		7		15		22
4th "	1		7		9		17
5th "	9		18		59		86
Grand total	10	:	54	:	92	:	= 156

Loss in 3rd Regiment by name: Corp'l W.E. Hinton & priv. J.R. Bedford, company A., wounded. L't W.T. Smith company B. wounded; Corp'l S.W. Phillips, E. Mears & Jno. Williams, company B., captured. L't T.H. Hall company C. wounded. 1st Se'g't. R.A. Singleton, Serg't T.R. Jordan &

W.B. Miller company C. captured. Cap't John K. Jones company E. captured. Se'g't Jas. H. Owen company H. wounded; E.S. Bailey, B.W. Conner & Jas. Faris company H. captured. Corp'l T.B. Johnson company I. wounded. C.H. Keech, A.M. Orgain & B.H. Spiers, company J., captured. Priv. Jas. H. Wilson company K. captured. Maj. Henry Carrington captured & Ser'g't Jas. W. Stith. Our sharpshooters getting a good position behind a rock fence saved the day when we fell back. The loss of the enemy admitted in one Regiment alone was 200 & in all must have been 300. After manoeuvering about till dark, we fell back to Goose County bridge, on the Little river turnpike and encamped for the night.

June 18: Started at 11 a.m. for Union, hearing that the enemy were moving from Aldie towards Snickersville, we marched to get ahead of them on the turnpike and drew up at a blacksmith shop, in one mile of Snickersville, to meet them, but they fell back a little before dark & we followed them up. 3rd Regiment encamped near Snickersville.

June 19: The enemy advanced a short distance from Montville. We moved down the road towards Aldie & encamped 2 miles from Snickersville. Rained very hard tonight & a considerable fight at Middleburg today.

June 20: Remained in camp today; enemy advanced somewhat, but soon fell back & we unsaddled. Late this evening ordered to saddle up & await further orders—went to sleep ready to move at a moment's warning. Day dark & cloudy, but little rain.

June 21: Enemy advanced in heavy force along the little river pike as far as Upperville, our men falling back before them in good order. Moved this morning at day break to Bloomfield & dismounted in a field nearby. Hearing that the enemy were advancing towards Snickersville, we returned nearly to the shop at said place, at night falling back to the Gap & encamping on the mountain. One Brigade of Hood's Division came up in the Gap & encamped ready to repel any advance of the enemy, should they try to pass through the gap.

June 22: Moved to Ebenezer Church near Bloomfield & picketed towards Union, connecting with the 4th Regiment on our right & the 1st on our left. At 4 P.M. reported that the enemy were advancing along the turnpike from Philemont to Snickersville. We moved towards said Blacksmith shop & the enemy ceasing to advance, we went into camp between Snickersville & Bloomfield, putting out pickets towards Union. 5th Regiment had a fight with the foe near Philemont & at least succeeded in checking them; one Major & 3 privates of said Regiment being killed & one wounded.

June 23: Remained in camp till this evening; then moved on Snickersville turnpike, when the whole Brigade moved back to Union & encamped at a church ¾ of a mile from Union towards Middleburg. Gen. Jones' Brigade went to Snickersville to relieve us.

June 24: At 11 a.m. moved out from camp near Union with 3 days' rations & marched by Upperville & encamped in a field near Salem, without unsaddling ready to move at a moment's notice, Fitz Lee's, W.H.F. Lee's & Hampton's Brigades being along.

June 25: Moved out at 1 a.m., passing through Salem & near White Plains & crossing the Bull Run Mountains by a private road in 1½ miles of Thoroughfare gap. The enemy, under Gen. Hancock, occupy this gap in very strong force. We captured several of their pickets here and they supposing us the advance of the whole confederate army, fell back rapidly towards Manassas & Centreville. Coming on the Warrenton & Centreville turnpike, we crossed the Broad Run at Buckland & went down the pike as far as Gainsville; but finding a heavy Infantry force of the enemy, we made no effort to pursue them. Camped at Buckland & some rain tonight.

June 26: Moved out early this morning, marching rapidly by Greenwich & Bruntsville & thence by Bristoe Station. Found that the enemy had gone up towards Centreville yesterday evening. Moved on towards Occoquan & camped at "Maple

Valley" at a place on the road to Dumfries. Had very poor grazing for horses, this being a miserably poor country & the armies having entirely consumed it. Sent out Capt Mathew's squadron on picket.

June 27: Marched out at 4 a.m. & crossed the Occoquan at Wolf Run Shoals; proceeded to Bank's Station & thence to a point on the Little river turnpike between Fairfax C.H. & Anandale. Part of the Brigade went to Anandale & captured some prisoners & sutler's stores. Distributed some cakes, crackers & c. to the command & then marched by Vicuna on Alex. Hampshire & Loudon R.R. and crossed said road at Hunter's Mill. Marching to Drainesville, we captured some prisoners and dismounted till after dark, when we moved towards the Potomac & crossed it.

June 28: Remained at a small village on the Chesapeake & Ohio canal till 6^1/$_2$ a.m. & while here a number of boats laden with army stores, came down. Had an excellent feed for horses & men & after destroying the boats, taking some mules & c, we moved off towards Rockville Md. The 9th Regiment being in advance, met a party of the 2nd N.Y. Cavalry on the road leading to Georgetown, & wounded severely ^{1}/$_2$ dozen of them & driving back the remainder. Getting on the turnpike from Georgetown to Hagerstown, Gen. Hampton captured a large number of wagons & advancing down the road to within 2 miles of Georgetown he took 175 fine wagons with beautiful 4 & 6 mule teams. Staying at Rockville but a short time, we moved out with the wagons, prisoners & c. to Mechanicsville & Brooksville. Here we were halted awhile from a false alarm that the enemy were ahead. Passed through & took the road leading to Unity & Westminister and continued on road all night without camping. Having heard that a party of the enemy were ahead, sent forward two Regiments to surprise & capture them, but they had themselves captured one of Gen. Lee's couriers & learning our proximity, fled. Passed through a beautiful & highly cultivated, though not very rich, section of country; the people having seen but little of war in this part of Montgomery county. Sent out & captured quite a number of horses from Union men, leaving our broken down ones. **June 29:** Crossed the Patapsco river & the Bal. & Ohio R.R. at Hoodsville. Having torn up a portion of the track & cut the telegraph wires, we moved most of the command one mile beyond to graze & wait for the train from Washington at $10^1/_2$ a.m. Gen. Hooker, having been relieved of the command of the army of the Potomac, was expected down (on train) this morning; but hearing that we were on the line, the train did not come. After waiting till $10^1/_2$ a.m., we marched for Westminster, Md. & reached this place at 5 P.M., 3rd Regiment being in front. Hearing that there was a party of 110 Yankees here, the 3rd Regiment was ordered to flank the town towards Hagerstown, while the 4th charged down the turnpike. The 3rd had to go so much further that it did not get up in time to prevent the escape of the Yankees by the Frederick turnpike. The 4th Regiment lost 2 killed & 5 wounded and we killed & captured 45 or 50 Yankees. Driving out the enemy, we occupied the town & got a good feed for our horses from the Western Maryland R.R. depot. The men got hats, boots, shoes & such things as they needed. We moved out, just before dark, on the turnpike leading to Gettysburg, Pa. and encamped at Union Mills on Pipe Creek, late tonight.

June 30: Set out for Hanover & met Gen. Stahl's command here. Gen. W.H.F. Lee's Brigade charged into the town & drove the enemy out but not being properly supported, he had to fall back before superior forces of the enemy. Our Brigade charged a party sent to meet us at Sherrystown & completely routed it, killing, wounding, & capturing quite a number. Sam'l C. Hubbard, company H. of this Regiment was slightly wounded in the arm with a pistol. Being broken down & in no condition to fight, we turned off towards Jefferson, Pa., which place we reached at $6^1/_2$ P.M. without any difficulty. We marched all night.

July 1st: Turning off to the left before reaching York, we halted at Dover about 8 a.m. & fed in the streets, the mules,

General Robert E. Lee
Virginia State Library

General J.E.B. "JEB" Stuart
Virginia State Library

General "JEB" Stuart's sabre, saddle, hat, and gloves
Museum of the Confederacy

Clifford Dowdey

horses, & men being much jaded. Found that Gen. Ewell had been here with his forces, but had left a few days ago. Great fight commenced today between Gen. R.E. Lee & the Yankees at Gettysburg. After halting here awhile, we set out by Dillstown to Carlisle. Hearing that the foe were there in considerable force, we advanced cautiously; but met with no enemy pickets before reaching the town. After we advanced very near to the town, the enemy threatened to charge. We moved forward rapidly to meet them, we found only a group of skirmishers. It being about dark, we opened on the town with our cannon & after firing a few shots, sent in a flag demanding a surrender, but the commanding officer refused & after waiting one hour, our pieces were placed in position & a terrific fire opened on the town. Having thus shelled it for some time, another demand was made, which was again refused. We then set fire to the Carlisle barracks, and some other buildings, which was a spectacle but for the suffering women & children they are our enemies. The town had been considerably battered. We spent the last night placing pickets along the Harrisburg road and we captured some prisoners attempting to escape. Before day, finding that it was impracticable to carry the town with our supply of ammunition, we moved off towards Papertown in the Cumberland Valley, where we dismounted & fed. Enemy made no effort to follow us. This is a beautiful little town near the south mountain pass. After grazing awhile, we moved through Petersburg & soon met with Gen. Jenkins' picket. What a pleasing assurance, to think that after so many days & nights of incessant toil, we were within our lines & there would be some prospect for rest, for at least one night!! Gen. R.E. Lee had a heavy fight with the enemy today near Gettysburg, driving them back several miles. Just as we were coming in our lines near dark, the enemy threatened to outflank us, but we moved up rapidly & then took position to wait for them. Remaining here till after dark we moved off & went into camp on the road from Hunterstown. What a pleasant night!! We got in our captures safely = 175 wagons, besides a number that were destroyed as they broke down on the road, 72 nice ambulances, 3000 horses, 1200 fine mules & 746 prisoners, men & horses very tired & hungry.

July 3: Moved out early this morning to Cunningham's X roads & thence to Hunterstown—grazed in a field near this place & then moved farther down on our left flank near "Granite Station", the enemy with cavalry & artillery threatening to drive in this flank. There was a heavy fight on this wing between several Brigades of our cavalry & a heavy force of the enemy—mostly sharpshooters & artillery engaged. We moved up to Hampton's support & he held his ground, though failed to take the enemy's battery. Only the 1st Regiment in our Brigade made a charge, though we were ordered in & the order was afterwards countermanded. However, the sharpshooters of our entire Brigade were engaged. The fight, for us, between the infantry near Gettysburg. We took a considerable number of prisoners, but our loss in attempting to storm the heights held by the enemy was very heavy, particularly in Pickett's Division. Remained near the Battlefield, in which the cavalry were engaged, till after dark, when we retired beyond Hunterstown, getting oats from "Granite depot" & encamped for the night. A very warm day.

Gen. Wade Hampton was quite severely wounded in the head & leg & the wounded in the 3rd Regiment are by name as follows: Cap't. G.W. White, Co. A., in foot; Lt W.T. Boyd, Co. A., slightly; Priv. P.H. Arnold, Co. A., missing; Corp'l R. Moore Co. A., slightly wounded; Priv. W.J. Yancy Co. C. & B.F. Jenkins Co. A. wounded.

July 4: Disagreeable rain all day & not much fighting today. We remained dismounted & saddled in a field near Cunningham's X roads. Gen. R.E. Lee having determined to fall back, after dark we moved down towards Gettysburg to cover the retreat of the army.

July 5: Remained very near the enemy's lines till nearly day, when we moved off on the road leading to Chambersburg,

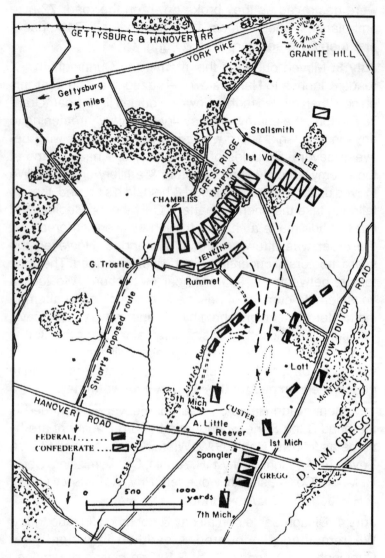

Cavalry battle at Gettysburg

Clifford Dowdey

Scene of the cavalry battle at Gettysburg showing location of
Stuart's guns pointing toward the Rummel barn

across the Blue Ridge. Disagreeable & heavy rain from 1 to
5 a.m. As we passed our late Infantry camps, quite a melan-
choly spectacle was presented. Stragglers, who had become
missed of their command during the night & who were throng-
ing the road, not knowing which way to go, & sick & wounded
men in large numbers, who must soon fall into the hands of
the enemy. Passed through New Salem & halted at
Cashtown to hold the gap till our train passed up. At 2 P.M.
we mounted & marched through the gap by Steven's Iron
furnace to Greenwood, where we turned off on the road to
Greencastle. This town Greenwood, is 8 miles from
Chambersburg. The furnace alluded to was the property of
the Hon Thaddeus Stevens of Pa., a notorious abolitionist
in Franklin County. His furnace had been destroyed by our
army. We halted here for sometime to graze—enemy came
in sight about dark, following us up, but advancing our sharpshooters, they soon retired. We then moved off & camped
in one mile of Funk's town, Pa. Some of the enemy's cavalry from Chambersburg & Mercersburg captured a portion
of our wagons—say 50—at Greencastle, together with some
men. Priv. R.A. Gregory, A. Griffin, R.W. Nash, W.E.
Robertson, & W.R. Ryan Co. A.; W.H. Wilburne Co. C.; W.H.
Harwood & J.M. Hubbard Co. D.; John Lee, Tagewell
Fitzgerald & Edward Phenix Co. E.; E.L. Adams Co. H. Wm.
Pomfrey & W.A.F. Jones Co. F. & D.A. Blanton Co. G. all
captured today with the wagon train near Greencastle.

July 6: Moved out at day break & after marching a while,
dismounted & fed at Brown's Mill in 3 miles of Greencastle.
Passed through Greencastle & halted for sometime at the X
roads leading to Hagerstown, Mercersburg & Williamsport.
Heard heavy cannonading towards Hagerstown, where Gen.
Stuart with W.H.F. Lee's & another command was engaged
with the enemy. He succeeded in driving out the enemy &
occupying the place. Our Brigade & Hampton's moved on
towards Williamsport & the enemy made a desperate effort
to take Williamsport with our wagon train congregated there.
Here the dismounted cavalry men & Infantry stragglers with

Gen. Imboden drove them back with heavy loss. Tonight we encamped in 1½ miles of Williamsport at Millville, with Potomac very high & past fording. Private O. Gregory Co. D. was severely wounded & priv. J.H. Bowery Co. D. was killed. N. Thackston & G. Hunt Co. K. missing.

July 7: Remained in camp nearly all day grazing our horses. Moved out at 1 P.M. towards Funk's town, Md. & encamped tonight near this town. Passed heavy forces of our Infantry on the right bank of the Antietam creek. Heavy rain tonight.

July 8: Moved out 7 a.m., in a heavy rain, for Boonsboro. Fitz Lee's, W.H.F. Lee's, Hampton's & Jones' Brigades came up with the enemy at Beaver Creek & drove them back gradually with sharpshooters; but coming upon a very heavy force of Infantry & learning what we wished, we retired a few miles & went into camp 3 miles from Boonsboro, having driven the enemy within 1½ miles of that place. Wagons ordered from Williamsport & Hagerstown. J.H. Hutchinson & Jas. H. Edmonson Co. A. and P.M. Nelson Co. D., were wounded. A total of 5 were wounded in the 3rd Regiment.

July 9: Enemy reported advancing early this morning. Moved out to meet them, but they made no effort to come beyond Beaver Creek till 5½ P.M., when they advanced boldly with a heavy force & we fell back 1½ miles towards Funkstown. Remained in a fine grass field all day until this advance. Went into camp near Funktown with F.A. Hundley Co. D. & R.K. Curtis Co. B. wounded today.

July 10: Moved out of camp early this morning to meet an advance of the enemy coming in heavy force. Pressing on us, we fell back rapidly to & through Funktown, but deploying our cavalry, Infantry & sharpshooters at the edge of the town, they were held in check. They poured a heavy artillery fire into the town as we passed through it, killing Se'g't Theophilus Foster Co. E. & private D.B. Ellyson Co. F. & wounding Se'g't J.M. Jeffries Co. G. After remaining on the hill west of Funkstown for sometime, we moved down the right bank of the Antietam creek to meet the advance of enemy from the direction of Sharpsburg. We met them in 1½ miles of Jones' X roads & after skirmishing a while—they having artillery & we none with us—we fell back ¹/₂ mile & put out pickets. Leaving Cap't Field's squadron on picket, the balance of the Regiment with the Brigade came back to camp on turnpike from Sharpsburg to Hagerstown. **July 11:** Moved out at 5 a.m. to support the squadron on picket, but our lines having been drawn in, we retired to a Dunkard Church & remained in a grass field all day. Our Infantry commenced throwing up breastworks on the crest of hills extending from Downsville on our right, to beyond Williamsport on our left. Hostile advance late this evening & our Infantry & sharpshooters retired before them. Heavy fight expected tomorrow. Camped on the road to Williamsport— 1¹/₂ miles from Dunkard Church.

July 12: Moved out at 12 M. & remained in column of squadrons for sometime & then went into camp not far from the place we stayed last night. Enemy skirmished a little, but made no serious advance, employing the day throwing up breastworks. They made a dash on some of our cavalry at Hagerstown & captured some of Gen. Jones' sharpshooters.

July 13: Several hundred men engaged in building a pontoon bridge at Falling Waters on the Potomac. Moved out today & went towards our left wing & then towards our right to Downsville. After dark we were ordered to re-enforce Col. Wickham & cover the retreat of our army. Gen. R.E. Lee having waited for the enemy several days & finding that they were throwing up substantial works, behind which they could retire in case of defeat, and besides, that they were indisposed to attack him, seeing too that he had exhausted his supplies in the territory then occupied, determined to recross the Potomac at Williamsport & a pontoon bridge at Falling Waters. We were ordered to put out pickets & relieve the Infantry pickets who retired at midnight. Very heavy rain tonight.

July 14: At 4 a.m. we moved at a pretty brisk pace to Williamsport, hurrying on some infantry stragglers. After waiting here awhile, we crossed the river with very deep fording. This evacuation, with a large army in front & a very deep river behind him, was conducted by Gen. R.E. Lee in such a masterly manner that the enemy knew nothing of it till late this evening & then they advanced cautiously, capturing a few stragglers & not a gun. They appeared in small force on the hills around Williamsport at 8 a.m. Our cannon from the Va. hills opened on them & a brisk artillery duel ensued. Our army seem to be very generally pleased at the idea of returning to Va. & seem to think they are at home & on hospitable soil in the "Old Dominion". We moved out to Hainesville, dismounted & grazed our horses a while & then marched through Martinsburg, Berkeley Co., Va., encamping at Newcomer's Mill. The county of Berkeley seems to be very poor—at least that portion on the turnpike from Williamsport to Martinsburg. This latter town appears to be very disloyal, being settled, to a considerable extent, by Yankee employees on the Bal. & Ohio R.R. Our army encamped all along this turnpike & towards Shepherdstown.

July 15: Moved this morning one mile to get grazing for our horses, going into camp for a while. We were fortunate enough here to get a few barrels of corn, though this county has been pretty generally devastated by both armies. At 2 P.M. marched via Leetown towards Rippon & encamped near the turnpike from Charlestown to Smithfield.

July 16: Moved towards Leetown & took the turnpike for Shepherdstown; came upon the enemy at Walpin's X roads & charged them, 1st Regiment being in front. They gave away rapidly & retreated to Dr. Boteler's, where being reinforced, they made a stand! Col. Drake of 1st Regiment charged them into the woods, but was forced to retire, being mortally wounded. They occupying these woods, our sharpshooters were ordered forward & artillery brought up. From this position they were slowly driven through the woods nearly to A.R. Boteler's house, where they made a stand behind a fence. Jenkin's Brigade coming up, they

were finally driven from this position. Night closed the scene
& putting out pickets; we retired to Mr. Schley's near
Walpin's X roads & encamped for the night. Heavy rain
tonight. The fight was very severe between the sharpshooters. Col. Jas. H. Drake 1st Regiment, was killed while gallantly leading his Regiment in a charge. L't W.S. Guy co.
E. was wounded; private Henry Robertson & J.P. Bennett
co. A. killed; R.H. Dabney, G.F. Marable & T.A. Walker co.
A. are wounded; B.E. Lepscomb & R.B. Harwood co. D.
wounded, & F.E. Cabell co. G. wounded.

Loss in the Brigade as follows:

	Killed	Wounded	Missing	Total
1st Reg.	2	8	0	10
2nd "	0	8	0	8
3rd "	2	7	0	9
4th "	0	12	0	12
5th "	0	0	0	0
Grand total	4 :	35 :	0 =	39

July 17: At $4^{1}/_{2}$ a.m. the enemy having retired across the
river during the night, leaving some of their dead & wounded
in Shepherdstown, we returned to former camp near
Charlestown & Smithfield turnpike, where we remained all
day & encamped for the night. Enemy's loss yesterday was
probably 75 or 100 killed & wounded.

July 18: Moved this evening to a new camp near Col. T.
Hites in Jefferson Co. near Leetown.

July 19: In camp quiet & a pretty day.

July 20: Quiet in camp. Cap't Matthews sent on picket towards Duffield's depot. Col's. Munford, Wickham, & Roper
came over to examine private C. Carrington co. C. for 1st L't
of co. H. & private Jas. W. Jordan co. H. for 2nd L't of same
company, both recommended by Col. Owen for said posi-
tions. They reported favorably.

July 21: In camp quiet & ordered to prepare 3 days rations.
Attended court of Enquiry with reference to defence of Kelly's

ford on the 17th March 1863. Cap't Jas. H. Allen of 5th Va. Cavalry & Cap't C.R. Irving of 1st Va. Cavalry, were on said court.

July 22: Started at 4 a.m. & marched by Berryville & Millwood—the enemy occupying Chester Gap, we moved on to within 6 miles of Front Royal, Warren Co., where all encamped for the night. Gen. Longstreet drove enemy's cavalry out of Chester Gap & passed through yesterday.

July 23: Moved out at 8 a.m. & crossed the Shenandoah by a private road at "Island ford" & passed on to "Happy Creek" station on the Manassas Gap R.R., where we dismounted for a while. We learned that the enemy occupied Manassas Gap & so crossed the Blue Ridge at Chester Gap, leaving Front Royal to our right. After crossing, we left the turnpike leading to Flint Hill & Gaines' X roads & turning to the left, marched across the Rappahannock & encamped late tonight. Jenkins' Brigade came up by a different road & wagon train went on to Gaine's X roads.

July 24: Moved out at 6 a.m. & dismounted for several hours in 1½ miles of Gaine's X roads. The 2nd Regiment being in front, skirmished with the enemy for some time. Declining to attack them we moved off via the X roads to Jenning's ford on the Hazel river. Left a squadron on picket at this place & moved down between Hill's mill & Rixey's ford, leaving another squadron on picket at the former place. Part of Gen. Hill's forces had a fight with the enemy near Thornton's river, whipping them off; but, having no cavalry, he killed only 12 & they carried off their wounded.

July 25: In camp, Chappell's & Field's squadrons picketing at Hill's mill & Rixey's ford. The wagons caught up today & went into camp near Botts place—Rain tonight.

July 26: In camp quiet, with 2 squadrons picketing. Got a load of corn from Culpeper C.H. for horses.

July 27: Moved camp this morning on the road from Rixeyville to Culpeper C.H. Enemy quiet along the lines, but reported to be laying waste the counties in their possession. Rain this evening & tonight.

July 28: In camp still, with heavy rain today & tonight.

July 29: Relieved by 12th Regiment in Jones' Brigade & moved camp to Rev. Mr. George's place near Culpeper C.H. Grazing indifferent & rain this evening.

July 30: Upwards of 60 men went home today on detail from the Regiment, (3rd) for fresh horses. In camp quiet & more rain.

July 31: Informed through scouts today that the enemy were moving one of their army corps all night on the road from Warrenton to Elk Run towards Falmouth. Supposing that their aim was to get ahead of us & obtain possession of the Heights above Fredericksburg, our brigade moved this evening at 5 p.m. & marched all night, crossing the Rapidan at Ely's ford & passing Salem Church at 2 a.m. Aug. 1st. We heard that they had not made their appearance in Stafford opposite Fredericksburg & so we went into camp. A beautiful night. We passed the extensive breastworks of the Yankees made during the terrific fight of Chancellorsville. Water at Ely's ford was very deep in consequence of recent heavy rains. The 3rd Regiment had to transport the artillery ammunition across on horseback to prevent it from getting wet.

Aug 1st: Enemy put down a pontoon bridge near Kelly's mill & crossed 2 Regiments since 1 a.m. Advancing their cavalry in heavy force, they engaged Hampton's Brigade under command of Col. Baker, driving him back to our infantry supports near Mr. George's, where they fell back rapidly. Loss in this Brigade 15 killed, 55 wounded, & 130 missing; among the latter were Cols. Baker of 1st N.C., Young & Black. Weather intensely hot.

Aug. 2: Hot day & in camp quiet. Hostile advance reported to be through Stafford towards Fredericksburg. The 4th Regiment sent out pickets today & the enemy placed one opposite ours at U. States ford, during the night. Nothing so far for our horses to eat but clover, which salivates them very much.

Aug. 3: In camp quiet & got corn & sheaf wheat for horses. Weather still intensely hot.

Aug. 4: In camp quiet & Court of Enquiry concluded today. Considerable fight between Stuart & the enemy today.

Aug. 5: Moved camp to a field near Taylor's & got a very pleasant place in the pines.

Aug. 6: In camp quiet. Hood's Division came down today from Virdiersville.

Aug. 7: In camp quiet & weather very hot. Rev. Mr. Mosley of Charloth preached for us in camp.

Aug. 8: Quiet & hot.

Aug. 9: In camp quiet & Rev. Mr. Mosley preached again.

Aug. 10: Still in camp & Cap't Matthews squadron sent on picket for 3 days. Regiment paid off by Cap't Palmer to-day—Very hot.

Aug. 11: Still in camp & very hot.

Aug. 12: A small party of 15th Va. Cavalry being across the river beyond Falmouth, fell in with a party of Yankees who killed one & captured the balance of said party. Last night several of Cap't Mathew's squadron crossed the river & captured 2 disloyal citizens & 2 Yankee horses.

Aug. 13: Cap't Chappell's squadron was sent today to relieve Cap't Mathews. Heavy rain this a.m.

Aug. 14: In camp quiet. This morning sent a scout of 20 men under Ser'g't Coleman co. G. to cross the Rappahannock river in boats and capture a disloyal citizen, who had been in the habit of guiding the enemy in Stafford. Being unable to find a guide on this side of the river, the party did not cross.

Aug. 15: Quiet in camp.

Aug. 16: Went myself to Fredericksburg to act as Provost Marshal of the town, having a force of 110 men for the purpose. What a commentary on war & the depravity it generates! That it should require such a force to keep a place quiet once noted for its hospitality & order.

Aug. 17: In camp quiet. Myself on provost duty.

Aug. 18: Regiment quiet in camp.

Aug. 19: Sent Field's squadron on picket.

Aug. 20: Regiment quiet. Private R.J. Tyree (co. B. 2nd Va. Cavalry) was killed in a fray on the streets in Fredericksburg this evening.

Aug. 21: Day of fasting & prayer appointed by the President. Rev. M.A. Davis of 4th Texas Reg. preached in Fredericksburg today. Regiment in camp quiet.

Aug. 22: Col. Owen started on scout with a detail of 200 men from the 3rd Regiment & Brown Maryland battalion; Camped for the night near Port Royal in Caroline County.

Aug. 23: Col. Owen succeeded in crossing his command by 2 p.m. & moved up the river through King George towards Falmouth. Reached this point at 11 P.M. & crossed the river, catching, near the ford, 3 pickets of the 5th Michigan Regiment & Custer's Brigade. He returned to camp late tonight without any loss.

Aug. 24: In camp quiet.

Aug. 25: Lot of detailed men started home for fresh horses. Regiment quiet in camp.

Aug. 26: Relieved as provost marshal by L't Payne of 4th Va. Cavalry. L't. Col. Morgan of 1st Va. Cavalry & myself started for Culpeper C.H. to report as members of a general Court Martial to try the case of L't Col. John S. Green of the 6th Va. Cavalry.

Aug. 27: Regiment quiet in camp.

Aug. 28: Still in camp.

Aug. 29: Quiet.

Aug. 30: Nothing new.

Aug. 31: Moved camp to Mr. Howison's near Hamilton's crossing.

Sept. 1st: Everything quiet.

Sept. 2nd: Nothing new.

Sept. 3: All quiet.

Sept. 4: Quiet & commenced punishing men by putting them on "the beat". This was something new & created quite a stir.

Sept. 5: Regiment in camp.

Sept. 6: Regiment still.

Sept. 7: Concluded court-martial case of L't. Col. Green, acquitting him of all the charges & specifications. Regiment quiet in camp.

Sept. 8: Started from Orange C.H. to return to the Regiment, the court-martial having adjourned sine die.

Sept. 9: Returned to Regiment today & everything quiet.

Sept. 10: Col. Owen left on furlough today, leaving me in command of Regiment.

Sept. 11: All quiet & had a squadron drill this evening.

Sept. 12: Reorganization of cavalry announced. This Brigade was assigned to Brig. Gen. W.C. Wickham & consists of 1, 2, 3, 4 Va. Cavalry Regiments. We were ordered today to have 3 days rations on hand.

Sept. 13: In camp quiet at Mr. Howison's near Fredericksburg. Rev. Mr. Conrad preached this morning.

Sept. 14: Gen. Wickham moved off with the balance of the Brigade, directing me to remain with my Regiment until all the commissary stores have been removed & the wagon train comes up from Port Royal.

Sept. 15: Moved off this evening to protect the wagon train, and camped for the night at Spottsylvania C.H., picketing towards Chancellorsville. Left L't Hill co. I. with 20 men, at Fredericksburg on picket & having 6 days rations for man & horse.

Sept. 16: Marched to Verdiersville in Orange county, reaching that place with the wagon train at 3 p.m. Encamped on the old turnpike one mile from Verdiersville. 6th & 13th Regiments came down tonight & encamped near us. Nothing of special interest—Enemy quiet. Gen. Hayes sent a party across the river at Raccoon ford & captured 31 of the enemy.

Sept. 17: Nothing stirring.

Sept. 18: Heavy rain—all quiet.

Sept. 19: The enemy crossed today & caught several of our pickets; Brigade moved out to meet them, but they having recrossed the river, we returned to same camp.

Sept. 20: Quiet. Rev. Mr. Conrad preached this morning.

Sept. 21: In camp quiet.

Sept. 22: Gen. Stuart had a fight with the enemy at Madison C.H. on our left. Wickham's & Lomax's Brigades moved up to Orange C.H. & thence to Barboursville, via Liberty Mills, to support Gen. Stuart, who took some 50 prisoners today. Went into camp at 10 P.M. at Barboursville.

Sept. 23: Moved out this morning at 6 o'clock in pursuit of the enemy, the 2nd Regiment being in front. Found that the enemy had destroyed everything they could, but they retreated so rapidly that we came up with & captured only 20 of their rear guard. They retired across the Robinson river at Locustdale & we having reestablished our pickets on said river, returned to Orange C.H. & went into camp at 11 P.M. The 2nd Regiment was the only one in the Brigade that was engaged & lost 6 wounded, but none killed. This was a very severe march.

Sept. 24: Moved out at 11 a.m. & returned to same camp.

Sept. 25: In camp quiet today. Brig. Gen. Wickham furnished me with 100 Richmond made carbines, which I tried & found serviceable except 9. They were issued to companies A., D, I, & E.

Sept. 26: Sent L't Palmore & 36 men to Fredericksburg to relieve L't. Thos. Hall on picket. Balance of Regiment in camp quiet & Col. Owen returned to duty this evening.

Sept. 27: In camp quiet. Mr. Conrad preached today.

Sept. 28: Regiment inspected by L't Col. Green very minutely. This evening moved camp to Walker's Mill to get grazing for our horses.

Sept. 29: In camp quiet.

Sept. 30: Nothing new.

Oct. 1st: Moved camp today to Mr. Fraziers farm in 2½ miles of Orange Springs. On the march Brig. Gen. Wickham's horse fell with him & hurt him quite seriously. He fell upon & bruised his left leg.

Oct. 2: In camp quiet. Sent L't Haskins co. K. with 36 men to relieve L't Palmore on picket at Fredericksburg. Heavy rain last night & today.

Oct. 3: Quiet.

Oct. 4: Nothing new. Preaching this morning by Mr. Conrad & this evening by Mr. Landstreet, Chaplain of 1st Va. Cavalry.

Oct. 5: Commenced drilling twice a day—mounted in the morning & dismounted in evening, with dress parade once a day.

Oct. 6: In camp quiet—Drilling.

Oct. 7: Drilling. Board of officers consisting of Col. <u>R.W. Carter</u>, L't. Col. W.A. Morgan of 1st Va. Cavalry & Maj. C. Breckenridge of 2nd Va. Cavalry, met this morning to examine L't Joel M. Hubbard co. H. for promotion from 2nd to 1st Lieutenancy. They also examined L't John Lamb for promotion.

Oct. 8: In camp drilling. Sent Cap't J.R. Christian with 36 men to relieve L't Haskins on picket at Fredericksburg.

Oct. 9: Moved out this morning at 7½ o'clock for Pisgah Church in Orange County. Went into camp near this place. Drew Gun slings & muzzle loading guns; also 17 Belgian muskets from L't Minnegerode today. The guns were distributed to Field's squadron & the Belgian muskets to Cap't Mathew's company. Encamped near Jeremiah Morton's place tonight.

Oct. 10: Regiment remained in the same place today & night. Enemy crossed in considerable force at Morton's ford this evening, capturing some of Lomax's Brigade on picket; they then retired before day.

Oct. 11: Col. Owen, in command of Brigade, moved out at $7^1/_2$ a.m. & crossed the Rapidan, the enemy retiring before us. Found them drawn up at Stringfellow's house & the 1st Reg. went up to charge being supported by the 3rd, but just as we came in 150 yards of the enemy's sharpshooters, we were ordered to fall back. This perilous maneuver of charging front under enemy's fire, produced great confusion in the two Regiments & they retired in considerable disorder. The enemy advancing, I deployed two squadrons of sharpshooters, dismounted along the fence, to protect the guns. The 4th Regiment supported by the 2nd charged the enemy on our left & fell back, Col. Owen, commanding Brigade, having his horse killed & Capts. Newton's & Williams of the 4th being killed in the charge. Iverson's Brigade of Infantry came up & our sharpshooters advancing, the enemy fell back towards Stevensburg. Here the enemy made a stand, placing their guns on the elevation towards Brandy & we charged them at Barbour's house. My horse was shot & being dismounted, I was captured. The 2nd Regiment which was to have supported us, was thrown into confusion by the explosion of a shell in their column & did not come up in time. But they arrived soon enough to relieve me & to check the enemy after they had driven back my men. I then got another horse & we pursued towards Brandy Station, driving the foe beyond towards Beverley's ford & Rappahannock bridge. But just then seeing a heavy cloud of dust in the direction of Culpeper C.H. & not knowing that it was Kilpatricks Division retreating before Gen. Stuart in command of Hampton's Division, & seeing that all were surrounded on three sides by the enemy, we fell back towards Stevensburg $^1/_2$ mile under a galling fire from the artillery. But we were soon relieved from our embarrassing situation & charged the enemy, whereupon he fell back

Confederate States

1863
Octo 11th To Hon Col W R Carter Dr
To value of horse killed
in action at Stevensburg Octo 11th
1863 $3 800.00

I certify that the above a/c is correct
& just, that the said horse was my
private property & was valued, when first mustered into service at
eight hundred ($800) dollars by a
duly appointed board of officers
as will be shown by the certificate of
the adjt. hereunto appended & that he
was killed in an engagement with
the enemy on the 11th Octo 1863. near
Stevensburg Culpeper Co Va.

W R Carter Lt Col
3rd Va Cavalry

Culpeper 20th 1863. I hereby certify that
the horse aforesaid was valued when
first mustered into service by a duly
appointed board of officers at eight
hundred ($800) dollars as shown by
the records of the Regt in my keeping
C. T. Hubard Jr Adjutant 3rd Va Cav

Certificate to compensate Lieutenant Colonel William R. Carter for the loss of his horse in battle

rapidly towards Rappahannock bridge. It now being dark, we came back & went into camp near Bott's place, the Brigade being very much scattered & disorganized. Loss in Brigade as follows:

	Killed	Wounded	Missing	Total
1st Reg.	1	18		19
2nd "	8	26		34
3rd "	0	5	4	9
4th "	9	40		49
Grand total	18	89	4	111

R.A. Puryear co. A. captured; Lt Jno. Wray co. B. captured; Priv. H. Cole co. C., T. Walker co. D. & R.W. Munford co. D. wounded. L't P. H. Fitzgerald co. E. captured; priv. B. Ford co. G. & D.L. Armistead co. K. wounded & private Pat Carroll co. D. wounded.

The enemy's loss in today's fight must have been 750 killed, wounded & missing.

Oct. 12: Moved out to Brandy to meet an advance of the enemy from Rappahannock bridge & after 12 M. marched to Jeffersonton crossing the Hazel at Starke's ford. Remaining here a while, we crossed at Fox's ford, it being about dark. The 3rd Regiment was in front & I charged across the ford & drove off the enemy's picket on the opposite side; dismounted my sharpshooters & occupied the heights overlooking the ford. Then after occupying the road leading to Warrenton Springs & Bealeton, the 4th Regiment & Lomax's Brigade crossed & went into camp on road to the Springs. Deploying Boyd's & Field's squadrons at right angles across the road to Bealeton, we went into camp near the ford. Se'g't J.B. Boone co. A. was accidentally wounded on the head tonight by one of his company, who was attempting to fire on a Yankee advancing upon him in the dark. After 3 o'clock tonight, the enemy withdrew from our front. Had nothing to feed horses on tonight.

Oct. 13: Marched to Warrenton early this morning by way of the Springs & after remaining dismounted a while in a field near this place, we mounted & moved down towards Catlett's Station. When near Cedar Run we came upon a large force of the enemy convoying a train. After exchanging some shots with them, it was deemed prudent to retire. Putting out pickets, we encamped tonight in 6 miles of Bealeton on Mrs. Horner's farm. Gen. Stuart got between two columns of the enemy with Hampton's Division; but lying down quietly during the night, he got out safely bringing with him 175 prisoners.

Oct. 14: Gen. Ewell advanced early this morning towards Auburn & soon became engaged with the enemy. Gen. Hill advanced by way of New Baltimore & Greenwich to Bristow. He had a considerable fight with the enemy, losing 500 men or more from Cooke's & Kirkland's Brigades & 5 pieces of artillery captured by the enemy & 2 pieces disabled. This was thought to have been a badly managed affair—the two Brigades having been advanced in line of Battle without skirmishers & Hill being too slow to occupy the railroad cut. Oh for Jackson to lead this corps! We moved early this morning by way of New Baltimore, Buckland and Gainesville, to Langley's Mill, on Broad Run, where we encamped for the night getting very good feed for our horses.

Oct. 15: Moved out at 12 M. in the direction of Manassas Junction & came up with the enemy to left of the Junction facing towards Alexandria. Deploying our sharpshooters, we drove them across Bull Run & finding them posted strongly in their entrenchments, we fell back taking position in our old entrenchments nearby. They did not advance & we, putting out pickets, encamped in a piece of woods to the left of the Junction, having nothing for man or horse to eat. The fight between our sharpshooters & the enemy's Infantry was quite heavy today. Privates A.S. Boyd, J.J. Smith co. A., R. Christian, R.B. Harwood & John Hill co. D. & W.H. Jolly co. I. were wounded.

Oct. 16: Remained at Manassas Junction today grazing horses. Heavy rain all day & a hostile advance late this evening. We went out to meet it, but the enemy retired across the Run again. Putting out pickets, we encamped in the woods to the right of the Junction. Gen. Stuart with Hampton's Division went off towards Gainesville on a scout.

Oct. 17: Moved out this morning towards Gainesville & stopped on Elli's place half way between Manassas & Gainesville, feeding our horses there. The enemy advanced this evening on turnpike from the direction of the "Stone Bridge". We went out on the turnpike to reinforce Cap't Randolph, commanding 4th Regiment, but the enemy fell back to Groveton & after re-establishing our pickets, we returned & went into camp on Elli's place. Enemy advanced on Manassas this evening & Col. Chambliss, commanding W.H.F. Lee's Brigade, fell back rapidly & in disorder to Bristow Station. Lt Lamb with co. D. went on picket tonight.

Oct. 18: At 10 a.m. moved to Langley's Mill & encamped. Late this evening the enemy advanced rapidly & in force, from Groveton, on Cap't Randolph, driving him back from Gainesville towards Buckland. Sent out Field's squadron to reinforce L't J.M. Jordan co. C., who was on picket.

Oct. 19: Heavy rain this morning & we moved out before day by Bristow and Catletts. Marching to Auburn, we found the O. & A. R.R. entirely destroyed from Cub run back to Rappahannock Station. At Auburn we turned off towards Buckland to strike Kilpatrick in the flank & rear as he was pursuing Gen. Stuart down the pike towards Warrenton. We soon captured the picket on the road to Greenwich and pressed on; but came upon a heavy force of the enemy stationed on the hills around Buckland. Dismounting our sharpshooters, we advanced, driving back the enemy & finally getting possession of the pike at Buckland. As soon as Gen. Stuart heard our guns, he faced about pressed the enemy from the direction of Warrenton. Kilpatrick was unprepared for this & consequently was considerably demoralized. But a force of Infantry & artillery, which he had as a support, held the position around Buckland until the greater portion of his command had retreated by. We pursued them across Broad Run & charged them twice, the 3rd Regiment being in front; captured a number of prisoners—mostly Infantry—but coming upon the advance of the first army corps posted across the road in the woods, we were compelled to retire, having several horses killed & men wounded. Many of the enemy's cavalry being cut off from the bridge & ford at Buckland, attempted to cross the Broad Run at a mill higher up the stream & some of them with their horses were drowned & a number killed & captured. This was quite a successful affair & particularly gratifying, as the braggart Kilpatrick was completely outgeneraled & badly defeated. Putting out pickets, we returned across Broad Run & encamped at Buckland. Our loss in the Brigade was 2 killed & 13 wounded. Loss in the 3rd Regiment by name: Corp'l. R. Moore & priv. J. Townes co. A.; priv. E.B. Hubbard co. D.; priv. W.P. Dupuy co. K. all wounded.

Oct. 20: Marched early this morning to Auburn & thence by three mile station on the Warrenton Branch R.R. & crossed the river at Beverly's ford. The river was very full & a good number of men got their feet wet. Artillery ammunition had to be brought over on horseback. We went into camp on Dr. Green's farm & the men were very glad to return, as they have had no rations for 4 successive days. I consider this the hardest campaign we have ever been engaged in; consequently men & horses were both very much exhausted. It has been a very brilliant campaign for the cavalry, as they took most of the prisoners captured. Prisoners to the number of 2436 were taken & 434 of these were taken by Gen. Imboden at Charlestown, as he moved down the valley simultaneously with our advance. Before leaving camp this morning private C. Dowdy co. G. was badly wounded by some one shooting about the camp. This abominable practice had become intolerable.

Oct. 21: Moved camp this evening to Dr. Wellford's place to get more convenient to water & better grazing.

Oct. 22: In camp quiet & sent off men on detail to get fresh horses.

Oct. 23: Beautiful day & quiet in camp.

Oct. 24: Rainy & disagreeable day. The party that was left sick & with disabled horses at Orange Springs came up today. G.P. Mayo enlisted in company G. today.

Oct. 25: In camp quiet & day very cold. Mr. Conrad preached in camp today.

Oct. 26: Quiet. Rev. Mr. Wilson from N.C. preached this evening—Enemy advanced on a party of our infantry & cavalry across the river at Bealeton. They were driven back, however, with a loss of 20 or 30 men killed & wounded.

Oct. 27: Rev. Mr. Wilson preached again this morning. Had a regimental Court consisting of Cap'ts Watkins, Christian & L't Jno. Lamb, in the case of Se'g't Jas. H. Owen co. H., charged with absence without leave. They found him guilty & sentenced him to be reduced to the ranks, to forfeit one month's pay & be closely confined & put on the ring four hours a day for 10 days.

Oct. 28: Took the Regiment on picket this morning to relieve the 2nd Regiment at Rappahannock bridge. Went by Brandy Station, drew corn, dismounted & fed near that place. Left Cap't Collins in command of camp today.

Oct. 29: By order of Gen. Fitz Lee we brought all of the Regiment back to camp except Boyd's squadron.

Oct. 30: In camp & had dress parade this afternoon.

Oct. 31: Rained this a.m. before day. Sent W.T. Harvy & six men to Fredericksburg to get up blankets & axes for the Regiment. Yesterday sent Yankee ambulance & wagons to Gordonsville to get them repaired. Very cold this evening & Regiment in camp.

Nov. 1st: Sent out 125 men & 10 officers to report to Col. R.W. Carter of 1st Regiment to go on a scout. Said party went to Kelly's ford & went into camp for the night. Sent L't W.T. Boyd with 50 men to report to Cap't Randolph of 4th

Regiment, who with 200 men was ordered to cross at Freeman's ford & dash around & recross at Beverly's ford. He did so without suffering any loss or capturing anything, as the enemy ran off so rapidly it was impossible to catch them.

Nov. 2: The detail of 125 men returned to camp this morning. Gen. Lee having sent across the river, found the enemy in too strong a position & force and so determined to abandon his scheme. Went myself to attend Division Court Martial at Kennedy's House.

Nov. 3: Cap't J.S. Jones having succeeded in getting his company "B" detached from the Regiment for the purpose of recruiting his company, started today to the Peninsula, via Richmond, for that purpose. Balance of Regiment in camp quiet.

Nov. 4: Beautiful day & Cap't P. Fontaine inspected Regiment today by companies.

Nov. 5: Division Court adjourned today by order of Gen. R.E. Lee, in order that the members might attend the cavalry review in command of their Regiments & companies. Gen. R.E. Lee reviewed cavalry corps today in a Field near Brandy Station—Grand affair! Stuart appeared in all his glory! Several men were very seriously hurt by falling from their horses in the mock charge.

Nov. 6: Beautiful day. Regiment has orders to have three days rations & be ready to move at a moment's warning. Capt. Mathew's squadron was sent on picket yesterday evening & Fields' squadron sent this evening to reinforce him.

Nov. 7: Beautiful day. Enemy crossed Kelly's ford & captured some of our men at that place; they likewise attacked our forces across the Rappahannock bridge & captured the most of Hay's & Hoke's Brigades after dark. Some out of those commands succeeded in fording the river and escaped. Our loss at the two places was between 800 & 1200 men; the loss of enemy supposed to be great also. This was

Camp Fitz Lee Cav. Div.
Madison County Va Nov 27 1863

I certify that Proceedings of Genl. W. H. Charles 3 Va. Cavalry
led to the 17th of November 1863 that
any indictment... been in attendance as witness
of a Genl. Courtmartial which convened at
Camp Fitz Lee, Cav. Div. near Culpeper Court House
Culpeper County Va Nov 20 1863 by virtue of
Special Order No 32 ... from Hd. Qr. Cavalry
Army Northern Virginia

Geo. W. Robie
Judge Advocate

a very unfortunate affair! Ordered to be ready to move out tonight at a moment's notice & so we packed up & sent baggage back to Bott's.

Nov. 8: Moved out this morning before day to Brandy Station & found that the Infantry had all moved & left their camp. After waiting here a while the enemy advanced about 12 M. & we fell back towards Culpeper C.H., making a short stand at Kennedy's house. Found Anderson's Division entrenching in S. Bradford's field. Gen. Roper had a fight with the foe in direction of Rixeyville & they continued fighting till after dark. We went into camp one mile from Culpeper C.H., on the Sperryville pike.

Nov. 9: Moved out this morning and turned to left towards James City, & at Bethel Church in Culpeper near Brown's Store. Night very cold.

Nov. 10: Moved out this morning crossing Crooked Run at Wayland's Mill & Robinson's river at Locust Dale. Went into camp near Dr. Slaughter's in Madison County.

Nov. 11: In camp quiet at same place, but had poor feed for horses. Enemy advanced to Robinson's river & put out pickets.

Nov. 12: Day beautiful. I went with Boyd's & Mathew's squadrons across the Robinson's river as a convoy for our forage train & got 4 wagon loads of corn. Left one wagon broken down & returned to camp at 11 P.M.

Nov. 13: Went to attend Division Court-Martial assembled, by order at Barnett's ford; Field's & Chappell's squadrons went as a convoy for the wagons going across the Robinson's river for corn. Regiment moved camp today to Mt. Zion Church in Madison county.

Nov. 14: Myself moved down to Barnett's ford to stay instead of riding back & forth, to & from camp. Dismounted men went up to Mt. Zion Church today.

Nov. 15: Rain before day this morning. Regiment moved camp to near a mill in Madison County.

Nov. 16: In camp quiet.

Nov. 17: Brigade ordered across "Swift Run" gap into the valley, to reinforce Gen. Imboden & check advance of the enemy on Staunton. Wagons crossed the Rapidan at Barnett's ford & encamped near Orange C.H. Regiment encamped near Criglersville in Green County.

Nov. 18: Hearing that the enemy had gone back after coming some distance up the valley, our Brigade returned to camp this morning, passing through Madison Court House.

Nov. 19: Regiment in camp quiet.

Nov. 20: In camp quiet.

Nov. 21: Sam'l F. Whitt's case was tried today at Barnett's ford, Rain all day.

Nov. 22: Beautiful day overhead. I & L't Jas. K. Roberts rode to Orange C.H. today & Regiments went on picket with its head quarters at Zion Church.

Nov. 23: Regiment still on picket & Col. Owen went on Court of Enquiry to Orange Springs.

Nov. 24: Regiment on picket still.

Nov. 25: Same.

Nov. 26: Regiment relieved this morning on picket, by the 4th & returned to camp. I was sent for tonight from Barnett's ford to take charge of Regiment. Brigade having crossed the Rapidan at Germanna ford. We moved off at 10 p.m. & crossed the Rapidan at Barnett's ford & marched along the old turnpike towards Morton's ford, going into camp late tonight—5½ o'clock a.m.—on Jeremiah Morton's farm. This march was exceedingly disagreeable, as the roads were very slippery & the weather quite cold & frosty. Met Ewell's Division tonight, under command of Gen. Early, moving towards Chancellorsville as we went down to replace them at the different fords. Reported that the enemy have crossed at Germanna & are moving towards Chancellorsville & Spottsylvania C.H.

Nov. 27: At 11 a.m. we moved down towards Raccoon ford to meet an advance of the enemy who have crossed at said place, found that they had crossed & occupied the hills on the south side of the river, on a line with Palmyra Church. As we advanced on them, they withdrew across the river & commenced shelling us from the Culpeper bank, which they kept up all day. At dusk, putting out pickets, we retired & went into camp near Palmyra Church on Mr. Morton's place. Private Wm. D. Price co. G. was wounded on the head by a stray ball; also one horse was killed & two wounded in the Regiment. Gen. Roper captured 100 ordnance wagons & some horses near Chancellorsville, coming up on the rear of the enemy. Gen. R.D. Johnston drove back the enemy from Locust Grove for several miles. Killing about 400 & wounding, say 1600.

Nov. 28: Rain today. Enemy crossed at Morton's ford this morning, but advanced only a short distance, seeming content with holding their position on this side of the river. We moved out & took the same position we occupied yesterday, putting forward sharpshooters. The enemy seem very sensitive to any approach upon Raccoon ford. Private Jas. A. Lamb co. D. received a bad shoulder wound this evening in the pits.

Nov. 29: Moved out this morning and remained in supporting distance of the rifle pits, being dismounted near Mr. Davis' house all day. Enemy recrossed the river, last night at Morton's ford. We got corn for our horses tonight from Orange C.H. & camped at same place.

Nov. 30: Again moved out & remained in supporting distance of the rifle pits. Enemy dashed across Raccoon ford, but were soon driven back. Private Pawhatan Hill co. I. was wounded in the thigh. Enemy advanced on Gen. R.E. Lee this morning & had heavy skirmishing.

Dec. 1st: Clear & cold & Brig. Gen. Wickham returned to duty today. Meade, despairing of forcing Gen. Lee from his position, crossed to the Culpeper side of the Rapidan; Enemy quiet at the fords today.

Dec. 2: Remained at same place today & heard (that) the enemy (had) recrossed the river last night.

Dec. 3: Moved out at 11 a.m. & marched by way of Peyton's ford on the Rapidan, to same old camp in Madison County.

Dec. 4: In camp quiet & got 5 lbs. of corn for each horse this evening—the only feed we have had for 36 hours—horses in a starving condition.

Dec. 5: Quiet in camp.

Dec. 6: Regiment went on picket with its Hdquarters at Zion Church. I made arrangements to buy me a horse.

Dec. 7: General Court Martial convened today at Walker's house in Madison County. Regiment on picket & nothing new.

Dec. 8: Regiment still on picket.

Dec. 9: On picket still, L't W.A. Moss' case came up before the Court Martial.

Dec. 10: Beautiful day & Regiment still on picket. Brig. Gen. Wickham with a part of the 1st, 2nd & 4th Regiments & W.H.F. Lee's Brigade went to Albermarle today; Maj. Randolph with 4 companies went to Fauquier to operate.

Dec. 11: 3rd Regiment relieved on picket today by Gen. Lomax's Brigade & returned to camp.

Dec. 12: Regiment went to Albermarle today, while I myself remained on Court Martial to dispose of cases in Lomax's Brigade.

Dec. 13: Beautiful day after a heavy rain last night. The court was invited over to Col. Walker's today to dine. Regiment encamped at Bocock's tavern in Albermarle last night & reached Charlottsville tonight.

Dec. 14: Regiment left Charlottsville for the valley today & crossed the Blue Ridge at Brown's Gap, going into camp at 1 a.m. near the foot of the mountains in Rockingham Co.

Dec. 15: Mounted soon after sunrise, passed near Port Republic & moved towards Harrisonburg, intersecting the valley turnpike 3 miles above Mt. Crawford. Moved up the pike & camped 5 miles from Staunton.

Dec. 16: Marched back & camped near M't Crawford—Hard rain during the night.

Dec. 17: Rainy day. Left camp early, marched through Staunton to Greenville & camped for 4 hours. Left here at midnight, the rain having ceased.

Dec. 18: Marched through Lexington and camped 8 miles beyond.

Dec. 19: Marched all day & camped tonight at Buchanan in Botetourt County.

Dec. 20: Moved through Fincastle and crossed the "Alleghany Range" & Craig's Creek; recrossed both & took the pike from Fincastle to Covington. In the saddle all night.

Dec. 21: Got to Covington at 11 a.m. & fed here.

Dec. 22: Marched all day, crossed the Jackson river twice & camped on Cow Pasture river at 10 p.m.

Dec. 23: Mounted up at sunrise, fed & drew rations at Goshen & camped for the night at Jordan's Springs. Averill having escaped we were returning to Staunton.

Dec. 24: Marched 17 miles to Greenville.

Dec. 25: Very cold & Regiment marched beyond Staunton, camping 7 miles below on the valley pike.

Dec. 26: Marched to Harrisonburg. Maj. Mason came down yesterday from Staunton to carry all the men for duty to the command. I having been on Court Martial, set out with 28 men to join the Regiment & camped near Wyer's Cave.

Dec. 27: Regiment marched to New Market. I myself crossed the North & South forks of Shenandoah at Port Republic & marching steadily all day in the rain, came up with the command tonight.

Dec. 28: Very rainy. Marched to near M't Jackson, and I was stopped by Gen. Fitz Lee in New Market, who suggested that, as he did not expect to do much by the move down the valley, I had better return to Charlottsville in order that the General Court Martial, of which I was a member, might go on. As I left the command with Cap't Mathews & returned to Charlottsville.

Dec. 29: Regiment remained in camp near New Market, it raining all day.

Dec. 30: In camp—cleared off today.

Dec. 31: Rainy day. Left camp soon after sunrise, crossed the north fork of the Shenandoah and Great North Mountains & camped in Hardy County at sundown.

1864

1864

Jan. 1st 1864. Cleared off. Regiment crosses the Shenandoah Mountains & camped at 10 P.M. 2¹/₂ miles from Moonfield.

Jan. 2: Rested all day & night.

Jan. 3: Crossed north & south forks of the South Branch of the Potomac and two small mountains, getting into Petersburg & Burlington pike 12 miles from Petersburg. Gen. Roper who was in front, captured 36 wagons. We then got in front & captured, without fighting, a small fort.

Jan. 4: Started towards Burlington at daybreak & reached there at 3 P.M. Took a few prisoners and burned some Commissary Stores, camping at Rigby at 8 p.m., with some snow falling.

Jan. 5: Started towards New Creek at 3 a.m., but marched only 2 miles & then returned to Burlington. Having fed, we resumed the march towards Romney & camped at dark, ten miles from that place, on the road to Brock's gap.

Jan. 6: Left camp at sunrise, marched towards Brock's Gap & camped at Baker's tavern. Roads very icy & weather intensely cold.

Jan. 7: Marched all day & camped in Brock's Gap, it snowing hard.

Jan. 8: Many of the cattle captured in Hardy & Hampshire were lost in crossing the mountains in consequence of the intense cold. Marched to Harrisonburg.

Jan. 9: Remained in camp all day.

Jan. 10: Marched to Brown's Gap.

Jan. 11: Marched to Charlottsville.

Jan. 12: In camp quiet.

Jan. 13: Same.

Jan. 14: Quiet in camp with small feed for horses.

Jan. 15: Nothing new.

Jan. 16: In camp quiet.

Jan. 17: Same.

Jan. 18: Quiet.

Jan. 19: Nothing new.

Jan. 20: Had a large military ball in Charlottsville tonight. Regiment quiet.

Jan. 21: In camp quiet. Every body interested in the report that the Regiment is to be temporarily disbanded in consequence of the difficulty of getting forage.

Jan. 22: Regiment disbanded today & each company except co. B. allowed to go home, on condition that they meet once every ten days at some central point and report to Gen. Wickham the number present & the condition of the horses. Great joy among the men at the idea of getting home for 4 or 6 weeks!

Jan. 23: I remain on Court Martial duty.

Jan. 24: Still at Charlottsville.

Jan. 25: Started to Richmond on my way home.

████

Feb. 7: Butler threatened Richmond from the direction of Williamsburg & late tonight I received a telegram from Maj. Gen. Fitz Lee, ordering me to report at once to Richmond as soon as the Regiment could be collected.

Feb. 8: Sent letters & telegrams to the different companies, ordering them to report at once to Richmond.

Feb. 9: Gen. Fitz Lee countermanded the order to concentrate the Regiment, the enemy having gone back from Bottom's bridge.

████

March 1st. Regiment ordered to concentrate at once through Adjt Hubard—at Richmond, the enemy under Kilpatrick threatening that place. They crossed at Ely's ford and moved by Spottsylvania C.H. to Beaver dam & Frederickshall on the Central R.R.

Mc'h. 2: I went to Burkeville & spent the night to receive any telegrams that might be sent me & to transmit them at once to the different companies. The telegraph office was ordered to be kept open all night.

Mc'h 3: Went to Nottoway C.H. & ordered L't A.B. Jones to start at 8 a.m. on the 4th for Richmond.

Mc'h 4: Sent my horse & servant along with L't Jones & I went down on cars tonight. Cap't Watkins with co. K. encamped tonight at the Junction & I made arrangements for foraging companies E. & K. on their way to Richmond.

Mc'h. 5: Reached Richmond at 8 a.m., found that the Yankees had gone back, having been unable to penetrate Richmond & that Cap't Mathews with co. G. had arrived two days before. Put up myself at the American Hotel & spent the day in making arrangements for collecting the Regiment. Cap't Mathews went into camp with his company on Salmon's place, 2^1/$_2$ miles from Richmond, on the Meadow bridge road & co. G. of the 1st Va. cavalry, under Cap't Southall, was ordered to report to me.

Mc'h 6: Company "E." came in this morning & went out to camp. I went to "Wilton" & spent the night.

Mc'h. 7: Cap't Watkins co. k. got in this morning & went out to camp. Myself went out this evening. L't Lamb with co. D. got in late this evening.

Mc'h. 8: Went to Atler's Station to look for a camp. Corp'l Vaughan co. B. with 3 or 4 men reported this evening.

Mc'h. 9: In camp quiet.

Mc'h. 10: Co. F. got in today largely recruited & co. A. under L't Boyd, got in this evening 70 strong.

Mc'h. 11: In camp quiet.

Mc'h. 12: Reported that Kilpatrick is attempting to return to Meade by way of King William & Fredericksburg. We moved out 750 strong—parts of 3rd, 4th & 13th Regiments—& encamped late tonight at Hanover Junction. No field officer but myself present with the command & but few company officers. Issued artillery & muzzle loading guns to the 3rd Regiment, say 250.

Mc'h. 13: Quiet in camp.

Mc'h. 14: 13th Va. Cavalry ordered to Hamilton's crossing today to relieve Young's Brigade on picket. I sent back a courier to inform all companies, coming to report to Wickham's Brigade, to return to camp at Meadow Bridge road to await my return.

Mc'h. 15: The Amelia troop of 1st Va. Cavalry, went to report to its Regiment at Orange C.H. Myself with the balance of the command moved back to camp on Salmon's farm.

M'ch. 16: In camp quiet.

M'ch. 17: Quiet. Drew 87 sharps rifles & distributed them in the command.

M'ch 18: In camp quiet.

M'ch 19: Nothing new. Commenced drilling skirmish drill & sabre exercise.

M'ch 20: In camp quiet.

M'ch 21: Quiet & Rev. Mr. Conrad preached today.

M'ch 22: Very cold today—commenced snowing & snowed all day & night, making it rough on the men & horses. I traded horses today, paying 1300$ boot.

M'ch 23: Quiet.

M'ch 24: Nothing new.

M'ch 25: In camp.

M'ch 26: Col. Owen went home on 4 days leave of absence, leaving me in command of the cavalry forces here.

M'ch 27: Mr. Conrad preached in camp today.

M'ch 28: The ground having dried, we commenced drilling today—had a mounted squadron drill this evening.

M'ch 29: Sent W.R. White co. G. under sentence of Gen. Court Martial, to Richmond to be placed at hard work on the fortifications, with ball & chain, for four months. Hard rain tonight.

M'ch 30: No drill today in consequence of heavy rain last night. Col. Owen returned to duty today & Cap't Watkins started to Orange C.H. to report to Brig. Gen. Wickham for duty.

M'ch 31: Resumed drill today.

April. 1st. Drilled today & quiet in camp.

Ap'l. 2: Heavy rain last night & snow all day today—Very unpleasant time in camp.

Ap'l. 3: Clear, but bad day under foot.

Ap'l 4: No long food for horses for six days. Rain this evening.

Ap'l 5: Hard rain all day & very disagreeable in camp.

Ap'l 6: Rained all last night & stopped this morning. Nothing new.

Ap'l 7: Moved camp out on Edmond & Davenport's farm near Mr. H.G. Taylor's—good camp & fine change.

Ap'l 8: Beautiful day. Mr. Conrad preached this morning & Rev. W.H. Christian from Richmond this evening—both excellent sermons.

Ap'l 9: Commenced raining this a.m. and continued all day. In camp quiet.

Ap'l 10: Wet day under foot. Nothing new.

Ap'l 11: I went to Richmond today to get some ordnance stores.

Ap'l 12: Had a Regimental drill this P.M. Telegraphed for wagons to come down from Hanover Junction, they being unable to get a sufficiency of forage there.

Ap'l 13: A beautiful day & I had Regimental drill again & dress parade. Wagons came up today. By special permit from Gen. R.E. Lee had an election in co. D. yesterday for 2nd Lieutenant. I superintended it & Se'g't T.F. Pallard was elected. Ordered to be ready to move towards Fredericksburg Saturday.

Ap'l. 14: Had Regimental drill today.

Ap'l 15: Inspected by Maj. Gen. Fitz Lee & W.H.F. Lee today.

Ap'l 16: Heavy rain today & did not start to Fredericksburg in consequence thereof. Got Chas. Smith & Wm. Cole, free negroes conscripted in Richmond, assigned to the Regiment as blacksmiths, by order of Secretary of War. Acted in capacity of Brigade inspector by order of Maj. Gen. Fitz Lee.

Ap'l 17: Snowing today. Started at 9½ a.m. for Fredericksburg, myself being in command of 3rd & part of the 4th Regiments. Camped at Ashland at 2 P.M. & got corn from the Depot for our horses.

Ap'l 18: Clear day. Moved out at 9 a.m. and marched to Chesterfield depot, where we camped. Drew one day's rations of hard bread & bacon for men.

Ap'l 19: Moved at 8 a.m. & marched to Guinea's by way of Cooper's Store—found the bridges washed away & seriously damaged by the recent high water. Very difficult crossing the Mattaponi, after which we camped 1 mile east of Guinea's. Capts' Watkins & Matthews and L'ts. Lamb & Jones went up to Orange C.H. to attend as witnesses in Col. Owen's trial.

Ap'l 20: Beautiful day. Moved at 10 a.m. marched to Hamilton's crossing, & went into camp on Mr. Alsop's farm—very good camp.

Ap'l 21: In camp quiet, with good grazing for horses. Went to Fredericksburg to make arrangements to have fish caught for the Brigade. Dress parade this evening.

Ap'l 22: Beautiful day. Gen. Lomax's Brigade came up yesterday from Ashland & camped on the other side of the Massaponax creek. Cap'ts Fontaine & Tebbs inspected the arms and accoutrements of cos. C.H, J.F. to ascertain the right of property of said arms & accoutrements. Had dress parade this evening & yesterday & today had 50 articles of war read to the Regiment.

Ap'l. 23: Sent Chappell's squadron & Field's Co. I. on picket for 5 days. Beautiful day.

Ap'l 24: Sent co. B. to reinforce the picket. Gen. Chambliss with his Brigade started to Orange C.H. today to relieve Gen.

Wickham. Sent privates J.W. Sturdirant co. I., W.S. Pallard co. D., C.L. Peddicord co.. B. and Se'g't W.F. Tynes co. H. to Maj. Gen. Fitz Lee to be sent to Richmond to put in the navy, at their request, they being dismounted. I rode around the picket line today, finding it very long. Went on part of the battlefield of Chancellorsville. What solemn thoughts passed through one's mind in viewing the scene of such a conflict!! Spent the night with reserve of the picket at Zoar Church.

Ap'l 25: Returned to camp today & sent priv. Frank Thompson co. A. to Richmond to be exchanged for priv. Bracey of 14th Va. Infantry, the former being unable to mount himself.

Ap'l 26: Beautiful day. Gen. Wickham started from Orange C.H. today & encamped at Parker's tavern & Gen. Lomax sent out pickets to relieve ours. Co. G. returned to camp tonight.

Ap'l 27: Sent priv. T.D. Williams co. I. to Richmond, he being transferred to Cap't Epe's company. Gen. Wickham got down with the balance of the Brigade & went into camp near the crossing. Everything quiet.

Ap'l. 28: Beautiful day & nothing new.

Ap'l. 29: Commenced drilling twice a day today & had Regimental drill this evening. Gen. Wickham went to Richmond today to attend Congress.

Ap'l. 30: Beautiful day. Had regimental court today = Cap't Collins, L't W.T. Boyd & L't B.W. Lacy in case of private Jno. L. Walker co. D. charged with theft & abandoning his post before being relieved. Col. Owen had his trial before the General Court Martial today.

May. 1st.

Hd. Qrs. 3rd Va Cav
April 30th 1864

General:

I have the honour to forward herewith a Roster of this regiment embracing all of the officers which it has had from the time of its re-organization – 25th April 1862 – to the present day. On a recent visit to your office I found that you had a very imperfect Roster of the regiment and Col. Withers requested me to have one made out as soon as practicable and forward it; so that the one in your office might be corrected. A few of the dates are not given, because not known but it is hoped they can be supplied by you –

I am General
Very respectfully &c. &c. &c.
W R Carter Lt. Col. Comdg

Letter from Lieutenant Colonel William R. Carter to Brigadier General W. C. Wickham. Near Hamilton's Crossing.

In late 1864 and early 1865 hundreds of discouraged Southern cavalrymen, many having lost their mounts, in rags and near starvation, made their way to Union lines to surrender in order to get food and clothing.

National Archives

Card 1

(Confederate.)

C | 3 Cav. | Va.

William R. Carter

F, Capt. John E. Jones' Co. of Cav.
(Nottoway Troop.)

Age 27 years.

Appears on

Company Muster Roll

of the organization named above, from Nottoway
County, Va.,

for Aug. 29 & June 30, 186_.

Occupation _Lawyer_

Enrolled for active service:

When May 27, 186_.
Where Stationers co. H.
By whom Self Ent.

Mustered into service:

When May 27, 186_.
Where Richmond
By whom Self Ent.

Last paid:

By whom _____
To what time _____, 186_

To place of muster into service 62 miles.

Remarks: _Home & Enfling Co. by_
Maj. Eslin Cation.

This company was successively designated as Captain
John E. Jones' Company of Cavalry; Company G, 3d Regiment
Virginia Cavalry; Company G and Company F, 3d Regiment
Virginia Cavalry.

The 3d (also called the 3d) Regiment Virginia Cavalry was
formed of independent companies which had been mustered into
the service of the State of Virginia for one year. It was transferred to the service of the Confederate States July 1, 1861, and
was reorganized April 25, 1862.

Book mark:

B. J. Wheale

(542) Copyist.

Card 2

(Confederate.) | 3 Cav. | Va.

Wm. R. Carter

Lieut. Col., 3 Regiment Virginia Cavalry.

Appears on

Field and Staff Muster Roll

of the organization named above,

for May & June 1864
to date , 186_.

of Commission, or Nov. 15, 1862
mental Appointment,

at or absent.

Remarks: _Wounded near Tre-_
vilians Station on Va.
R.R. 11 June 1864. Died
of wounds 8 July, 1864.

M (also called the 3d) Regiment Virginia Cavalry was
formed of independent companies which had been mustered into
the service of the State of Virginia for one year. It was transferred to the service of the Confederate States July 1, 1861, and
was reorganized April 25, 1862.

Book mark:

L. Caxton

(646) Copyist.

Card 3

(Confederate.)

C | 3 Cav. | Va.

W. R. Carter

Col. 3 Reg't Va. Cav.

Appears on a

Report of Sick and Wounded

in   General Receiving Hospital
(also known as Charity Hospital),
at   Gordonsville, Va.,

for the week ending July 14, 1864

Disease Vul. Sclopt.

Admitted June 14, 186_.

Furloughed 186_.

Transferred to 186_.

Returned to duty 186_.

Died July 8, 186_.

Remarks:

Book mark:

J. B. Hyatt

(646) Copyist.

—*Part II*—

Part II

Battle of Trevilian Station

Let us review briefly the major aspects of the battle that took place at Trevilian Station in Louisa County on June 11 and 12, 1864, forty-five miles northwest of Richmond, in which Lieutenant Colonel William R. Carter was mortally wounded.

Over the years, historians, writers, and students of the War Between the States have failed to give the Battle of Trevilians the attention, publicity, or recognition that this military engagement deserves. Accordingly, public awareness of its importance is limited. Little has been published about this fight, a cavalry encounter fought mostly by dismounted troops. Firepower, as usual, favored the bluecoats with their Spencer repeating rifles.

Lieutenant General Ulysses S. Grant, President Abraham Lincoln's Commander of the Federal Army, on May 26, 1864, sent Major General David Hunter up the Shenandoah Valley with 18,000 men to pillage, burn, and wreak destruction in the Valley which was General Robert E. Lee's main source of food and supplies for his army. These military necessities were shipped over the Virginia Central Railroad through Charlottesville, Gordonsville, and Louisa to Richmond and Petersburg battle areas. Hunter's primary objective was to capture Lexington and Lynchburg where he expected to cut the James River Canal and the Southside Railroad, which led to Richmond, and go on to Charlottesville and make contact with Major General Philip Sheridan.

In the battles on June 11 and 12 Sheridan lost 93 men and nine officers; 438 men and thirty-two officers were wounded and 427 men and eight officers were captured or missing—for a total of 1,007 casualties.

Hampton's losses are difficult to determine. The official report off his operations June 8–24, 1864, states that in his division alone he lost 59 killed, 258 wounded, and 295 missing in the two days at Trevilians. There is no record of Fitz Lee's losses. It is estimated that his were about 75 percent of Hampton's and if the assumption is correct we must add 459 casualties to Hampton's total of 612, making a total of 1,071,

which is 64 greater than Sheridan's loss. This would
represent a loss of over 20 percent of the Confederate
strength compared to 12 percent of the Union.

On the first day of the battle there was a series of
charges and countercharges by both Union and Confederate forces in the vicinity of the railroad station.
The following day, Sunday, Sheridan made seven force-
ful charges against the Confederate defensive line in
the area around the Ogg house on the road to
Gordonsville. Each time the advances were repulsed
with heavy losses.

It was ten o'clock on the night of the twelfth when
the final fighting ended. Sheridan, believing that Confederate General John Breckinridge was at Charlottesville
and had re-enforced Hampton during the night and in
view of his heavy losses and shortage of ammunition,
decided it was unwise to try to join Hunter. After destroying several miles of railroad track he withdrew his
troops shortly after midnight, camping across the North
Anna at Twyman's Store.

Because of the condition of Hampton's men and
horses no move was made to pursue Sheridan until
daylight at which time scouting parties were sent out
to keep in touch with the retreating enemy.

On Monday morning Hampton sent Captain
Zimmerman Davis, Commander of the Second Squadron of the 5th South Carolina, to scour the battlefields,
bury the dead, look after any wounded and gather up
such abandoned arms as could be of service. Davis
found that Sheridan had left behind him three hospi-
tals with ninety Union soldiers and many Confeder-
ates. He also left a supply of medicines, liquor,
hardtack, coffee, and sugar. Assistant Surgeon Sickler
of the 10th New York and several attendants were car-
ing for those left behind. Residents in the area treated
all the wounded with tender care and all those who

could be moved were brought to the railroad and taken to the Gordonsville hospital in construction cars which had no springs and were open to the weather. The wounded, clad in blue and gray, waited patiently for the cars and were ministered to by the women of the neighborhood who brought with them whatever meager supplies and bandages that were left to them.

Let us now assess the results accomplished by Hampton and Sheridan in the clash of arms along the Virginia Central Railroad in the countryside of Central Virginia on those two hot days in June of 1864.

Sheridan's plan was to (1) join Hunter at Charlottesville, destroy the Rivanna bridge there, (2) tear up the railroad from that point to Gordonsville, and (3) keep the Confederate cavalry fully occupied while the Army of the Potomac delicately maneuvered east and south of Richmond in an attempt to take Petersburg and invest Richmond from the south. Sheridan did not meet Hunter, was not closer than thirty miles from Charlottesville and did only minor damage to the railroad. He was successful, however, in keeping General Robert E. Lee's two divisions of cavalry fully occupied, making it possible for Grant to move his base and army undetected and unimpeded.

In a report to Grant's chief of staff on June 16 Sheridan gives his reasons for not advancing further towards Charlottesville and concludes by saying, "I regret my inability to carry out your instructions."

Despite facing superior firepower and numbers of the enemy, Hampton had achieved the greatest victory of his distinguished career.

It is a very intriguing question as to why this outstanding and exciting diary of Lt. Col. William R. Carter was abruptly ended on May 1, 1864, just a few weeks before its author died in defense of his country.

NOTHING CAN SURPASS THE
WORDS OF THE MAN WHO WAS THERE!

Illustrations, pictures, and maps have been added to enhance the story's content.

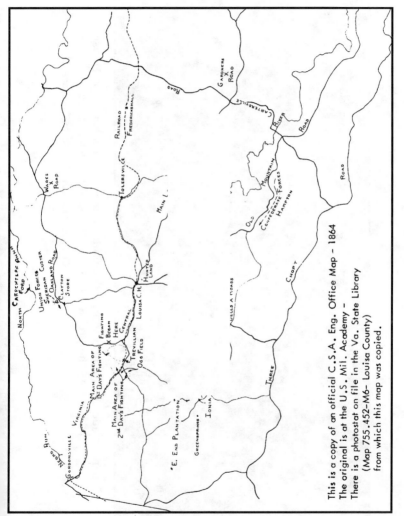

Louisa County, 1864

This is a copy of an official C.S.A. Eng. Office Map – 1864
The original is at the U.S. Mil. Academy –
There is a photostat on file in the Va. State Library
(Map 755.452-M6- Louisa County)
from which this map was copied.

General Wade Hampton leading "The Cadet Charge" at Louisa Court House which was the prelude to the Battle of Trevilian Station

Courtesy of the Archives Museum, The Citadel, Charleston, S.C.

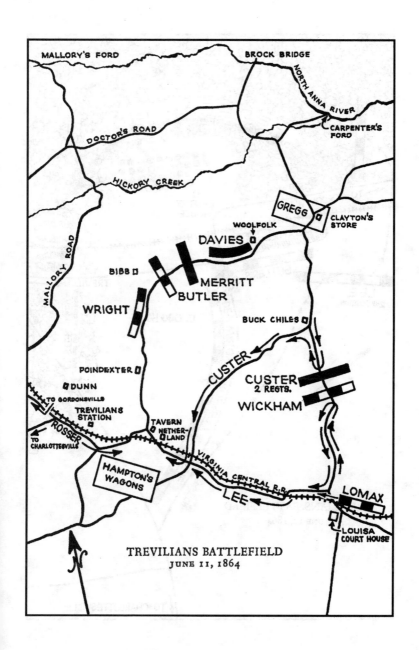

TREVILIANS BATTLEFIELD
JUNE 11, 1864

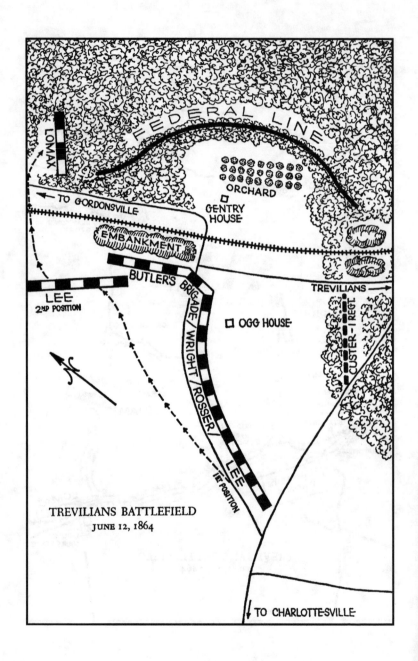

FEDERAL LINE

LOMAX

ORCHARD

GENTRY HOUSE

← TO GORDONSVILLE

EMBANKMENT

BUTLER'S BRIGADE

LEE
2ND POSITION

TREVILIANS →

OGG HOUSE

WRIGHT / ROSSER / LEE
1ST POSITION

CUSTER – I REGT

N

TREVILIANS BATTLEFIELD
JUNE 12, 1864

↓ TO CHARLOTTESVILLE

Organization of the Confederate and Union Forces

CAVALRY CORPS

HAMPTON'S DIVISION

Maj. Gen. Wade Hampton

Young's Brigade

Col. G.J. Wright

7th Georgia, Col. William P. White
Cobb's (Georgia) Legion, Col. G.J. Wright
Phillips (Georgia) Legion, Lt. Col. Wm.
  W. Rich
20th Georgia Battalion, Lt. Col. John
  M. Millen
Jeff. Davis (Mississippi) Legion, Col.
  J.F. Waring

Rosser's Brigade

Brig. Gen. Thomas L. Rosser

7th Virginia, Col. Richard H. Dulany
11th Virginia, Col. O.R. Funsten
12th Virginia, Lt. Col. Thomas B. Massie
35th Virginia Battalion, Col. Elijah V.
  White

Butler's Brigade

Brig. Gen. Matthew C. Butler

4th South Carolina, Col. B. Huger Rutledge
5th South Carolina, Jam. John H. Morgan
6th South Carolina, Col. Hugh K. Aiken

FITZHUGH LEE'S DIVISION

Maj. Gen. Fitzhugh Lee

Lomax's Brigade

Brig. Gen. Lunsford L. Lomas

5th Virginia, Col. Henry C. Pate
6th Virginia, Col. John S. Green
15th Virginia, Col. Charles R. Collins

Wickham's Brigade

Brig. Gen. Williams C. Wickham

1st Virginia, Lt. Col. Wm. A. Morgan
2nd Virginia, Col. Thomas T.
  Munford
3rd Virginia, Col. Thomas H. Owen
4th Virginia, Col. Wm. B. Wooldrige

HORSE ARTILLERY

Maj. R. Preston Chew
Maj. James Breathed

Hart's South Carolina Battery
Johnston's Virginia Battery
Thomson's Virginia Battery

CAVALRY CORPS

Maj. Gen. Philip H. Sheridan

ESCORT

6th United States, Capt. Ira W. Cladin

FIRST DIVISION

Brig. Gen. Alfred T.A. Torbert

First Brigade

Brig. Gen. George A. Custer

1st Michigan, Lt. Col. Peter Stagg
5th Michigan, Col. Russell A. Alger
6th Michigan, Maj. James H. Kidd
7th Michigan, Maj. Alexander Walker

Second Brigade

Col. Thomas C. Devin

4th New York, Lt. Col. William R. Parnell
6th New York, Lt. Col. William H. Crocker
9th New York, Lt. Col. George S. Nichols
17th Pennsylvania, Lt. Col. James Q. Anderson

Reserve Brigade

Brig. Gen. Wesley Merritt

19th New York (1st Dragoons), Col. Alfred Gibbs
6th Pennsylvania, Maj. William P.C. Treichel
1st United States, Capt. Nelson B. Sweitzer
2nd United States, Capt. Theophilus F. Rodenbough
5th United States, Capt. Abraham K. Arnold

SECOND DIVISION

Brig. Gen. David McM. Gregg

First Brigade

Brig. Gen. Henry E. Davies, Jr.

1st Massachusetts, Lt. Col. Samuel E. Chamberlain
1st New Jersey, Lt. Col. John W. Kester
10th New York, Maj. M. Henry Avery
1st Pennsylvania, Col. John P. Taylor

Second Brigade

Col. J. Irving Gregg

2nd Pennsylvania, Lt. Col. Joseph P. Brinton
4th Pennsylvania, Lt. Col. George H. Coyode
8th Pennsylvania, Col. Pernock Huey
13th Pennsylvania, Maj. Michael Kerwin
16th Pennsylvania, Lt. Col. John K. Robison

HORSE ARTILLERY

1st United States Battery H and I, Lt. Edward Heaton

2nd United States Battery D, Lt. Edward B. Williston

2nd United States Battery M, Lt. Alexander C.M. Pennington, Jr.

**General
Wade Hampton**

Virginia State Library

**General
Matthew C. Butler**

Virginia State Library

**General Fitzhugh Lee,
Nephew of Robert E. Lee**

Virginia State Library

134

**General
Lunsford L. Lomax**

Virginia State Library

**General
Thomas L. Rosser**

Virginia State Library

**General
William Carter Wickham**

Virginia State Library

Major General Philip Sheridan and staff. *Left to right,* Sheridan, Generals George A. Forsythe, Wesley Merritt, Thomas C. Devin, and George A. Custer. *Inset upper left,* David McM. Gregg. *Upper right,* Alfred T.A. Torbert.

The above picture illustrates the cavalry's method of destroying railroads. The rails were placed across piles of ties. When the ties were fired the metal got hot and because of the weight they bent out of shape. Note the tangle of telegraph lines which were also torn up.

Collection of Trevilian Station battlefield artifacts collected by Elton H. Strong of Mineral, Virginia

The Editor

Gordonsville Receiving Hospital

Mortally wounded, Lieutenant Colonel William R. Carter was taken to this hospital from the battlefield at Trevilian Station.

Exchange Hotel and Civil War Museum

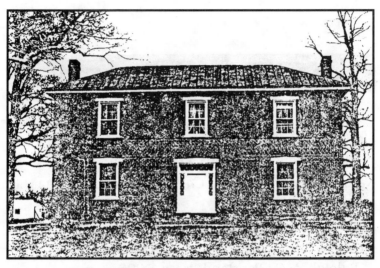

"Hickory Hill," home of Lieutenant Colonel William R. Carter

Bibliography

McClellan, H. B. *I Rode With "JEB" Stuart.* Bloomington, Ind.: Indiana University Press, 1969.

Nanzig, T P. *3rd Virginia Cavalry.* Lynchburg, Va.: H.E. Howard, Inc.

National Archives, Washington, D.C.

Swank, Walbrook D. *Clash of the Sabres, Blue and Gray.* Raleigh, N.C.: Pentland Press, 1996.

———. *Battle of Trevilian Station.* Shippensburg, Pa.: White Mane Pub. Co., 1994.

Wallace, Lee A., Jr. *A Guide to Virginia Military Organizations, 1861-65.* Lynchburg, Va.: H.E. Howard, Inc., 1959.

U.S. War Department. Official Records. Washington, D.C. 1880-1891.

Index

First names were listed where known.

139